PARTNERS IN
PRESERVATION

HOW TO KNOW YOUR ADVISOR
IS TRULY PROTECTING YOUR WEALTH

MO LIDSKY

Partners in Preservation: How to Know Your Advisor Is Truly Protecting Your Wealth

Published by Gatekeeper Press
2167 Stringtown Rd, Suite 109
Columbus, OH 43123-2989
www.GatekeeperPress.com

The cover design, interior formatting, typesetting, and editorial work for this book are entirely the product of the author. Gatekeeper Press did not participate in and is not responsible for any aspect of these elements.

ISBN (hardcover): 9781662901799

*As to methods, there may be a million and then some,
but principles are few. The man who grasps principles can
successfully select his own methods. The man who tries methods,
ignoring principles, is sure to have trouble.*

—Ralph Waldo Emerson

CONTENTS

ACKNOWLEDGMENTS

It is difficult to express the extent of my gratitude to all the individuals who helped make this book a reality. Firstly, I am deeply grateful to my partners and colleagues at Prime Quadrant. Thank you to Jeremy Rosmarin and Davee Gunn for challenging me to refine my investment philosophy, encouraging me to accept nothing short of excellence, and for inspiring many of the insights in this book. A heartfelt thank-you goes to all the dear friends and colleagues who have offered their critiques on the ideas within. They include, in no particular order, Michael Lax, Stuart Schipper, David Latner, Diana Pandya, David Kaufman, Reva Luft, Reeve Serman, Terry Vaughan, Tessa MacNeil, Wayne Nates, Karolina Kosciolek, Mori Oren, Mell Matlow, Julia Shuchat and Isaac Lempriere. Most notably, I am eternally grateful to my partner, mentor, and friend, Ian Rosmarin, whose decades of experience, wisdom, and advice have permeated every facet of investment acumen that I (and so many others) possess today.

I would be remiss if I didn't also acknowledge a debt of gratitude to our clients at Prime Quadrant, whose ongoing questions and curiosities enlighten us as much as, if not more than, we educate them.

Last but not least, thank you to my beautiful wife, Naomi, whose patience and support have been unbounded. She has endured my late nights at the office, alarms before the break of dawn, and frequent absences with writing, researching, and editing into the wee hours of the night. Through it all, she has masterfully managed a busy household of four amazing (and adorably menacing) children and has miraculously kept me physically and spiritually nourished throughout. How she does it all, I will never know.

DISCLAIMER

This book is designed to provide information on investment advice and investing best practices for high-net-worth families and individual investors. It is sold with the understanding that the publisher and author are not engaged in rendering any legal or accounting professional services. If legal or other expert assistance is required, the services of a competent professional should be sought. It is not the purpose of this book to provide all of the information that is otherwise available to authors and/or publishers, but instead to complement, amplify and supplement other texts. You are urged to read all of the available material, learn as much as possible about your investment options, and tailor the information to your individual needs. The ideas in this book do not provide any get-rich-quick schemes. Anyone who wishes to pursue a course of action consistent with the ideas presented in this book must expect to invest considerable time and effort in order to do so. Every effort has been made to make this book as complete and as accurate as possible. However, there may be mistakes, both typographical and in content. Therefore, this text should be used only as a general guide and not as an ultimate source of investing information. Furthermore, this book contains information on investing best practices that is current, only up to the date of printing. The purpose of this book is to educate and entertain. The author shall incur neither liability nor responsibility to any person or entity with respect to any loss or damage caused, or alleged to have been caused, directly or indirectly, by the information contained in this book.

INTRODUCTION

AHHHH! I have hung my hat in an industry that makes me want to scream. Not a scream of anger but one of exasperation. *How in the world are investors tolerating this? How are people paying for this garbage? How are they so satisfied with mediocrity, or worse?*

Quite frankly, I am fed up. I've seen enough misleading advertising. I'm tired of products that have so many piles of fees it makes your head spin. The aggressive marketing habits nauseate me. The inflated titles of salespeople only exacerbate the smoke and mirrors of the sector. I'm frustrated with the pitiable disclosures, confusing jargon, and heaps of inferior financial products. And don't get me started on the conflicts of interest. In our sector, it is at a level that is simply deplorable.

Most of all, I'm infuriated that all this is under the banner of—the one thing that should protect you against all of the above—investment advice.

This book will attempt to tackle candidly and unabashedly the myths and realities of financial advice. It will focus on the challenges of getting good help, how to access it, what to avoid, and what could be expected.

I am hopeful that the ideas in this book will help raise the bar of the industry so that investors can be better served and that well-intentioned advisors can be better equipped to support them.

Caveat Lector

You should be forewarned. What you will find in the pages ahead is not sexy. It is not enthralling. It may even appear somewhat boring. The reality is that investing, when done right, is somewhat boring. The goal is not to have something to talk about over cocktails with your friends; it's not meant to be exotic or entertaining. In fact, research suggests that where there are entertaining or sexy invest- ments, there are built-in premiums and diminished returns.[1] These pages will simply help you make better investment decisions and ulti- mately meet your financial goals. No more and no less.

This book may not make me any friends. In fact, after the pub- lication of a previous book, *In Search of the Prime Quadrant: The Quest for Better Investment Decisions*, I received several calls and e- mails from irritated brokers who said that we were too harsh on them and unnecessarily critical of their methods. But the truth is that there are many individuals and institutions that benefit from the neglect or ignorance of the vast majority of investors. They are only too happy for the gravy train to continue. I am not concerned about displeasing any of these individuals. My aspiration with this book is simply to help private investors with a candid analysis of the world of financial advice and how to best utilize it (or, in some cases, avoid it) to become better stewards of wealth and have the highest probability of meeting financial goals.

This book will prove to be particularly useful to affluent investors, their trusted advisors, accomplished entrepreneurs who are considering the next phase of their lives (away from the business), and anyone passionate about investing. To be clear, the investor I reference throughout the book is wealthy. He or she has investable assets rang- ing from a few million to several hundred million dollars. Though the insights in this book are useful for all, it is this group that will be its greatest beneficiaries. By contrast, those with less than a few million dollars may not have a choice but to deplete some or all their capital to sustain themselves in retirement and cannot afford top-caliber financial advice. At the other end of that spectrum, those with billions of dollars or even several hundred million dollars can often live off the risk-free rate of return and may not have a need to take any risk by investing. The individuals in the middle, however, are reliant on their capital and have a fair shot at preserving it for the next generation or some other worthy purpose. They have sufficient means to live on but must avoid any substantial loss of capital.

Throughout the book, I will address both investors and advisors because it is my fundamental belief that while advisors may be more involved in the portfolio, investors should never abandon their own stewardship responsibilities. No matter how honest and capable the advisor may be, he or she has less to lose than the investor, and therefore investors must dutifully accept their responsibilities as equal partners in preservation. The primary purpose of this book will be to outline how to optimize that partnership, helping individuals and families make better investment decisions.

PART I

INVESTMENT ADVICE

No enemy is worse than bad advice.

—Sophocles

Stay Rich

On January 4, 1877, Americans mourned the death of an extraordinary philanthropist, entrepreneur, the shipping and railroad tycoon, Cornelius "Commodore" Vanderbilt. By some estimates, Vanderbilt amassed the equivalent of $185 billion in today's dollars.[1] He controlled over 1 percent of America's GNP and was arguably the second-wealthiest person in American history.[2] Upon his passing, his entire estate was bequeathed to his children. That inheritance was greater than all the assets held by the US Treasury at the time. However, when 120 direct descendants of Cornelius Vanderbilt met at Vanderbilt University in 1973 for a family reunion, they were surprised to find that there was not a single millionaire among them.[3]

There is no shortage of research demonstrating that family wealth rarely survives the intergenerational transfer. Over 70 percent tends to evaporate by the end of the second generation and more than 90 percent by the third.[4] But it is not just inheritors that experience spectacular downturns. Even self-made entrepreneurs are often poor stewards of the wealth they may have spent a lifetime building. There are dramatic stories of individuals like Halsey Minor, who sold CNET Networks in 2008 for nearly $2 billion and in May of 2013 filed for bankruptcy. This Charlottesville, Virginia, native was a pioneer in tech start-ups and cloud computing, cofounding the likes of Salesforce.com, Rhapsody, NBCi, and Google Voice. However, through a combination of bad investments and irresponsible spending, the fruits of these successes quickly become a distant memory.

Minor's story is not unique. Eike Batista was once the eighth-richest person in the world, and by far the wealthiest Brazilian, with a fortune of over $30 billion. But between the spring of 2012 and the summer of 2013, Batista's wealth was reduced to less than 1 percent of its former grandeur. In Ireland, there is Seán Quinn, once Ireland's wealthiest person with a net worth of over $6 billion, who was declared bankrupt on January 16, 2012. In Iceland, there is Björgól-fur Guðmundsson, the former chairman of Landsbanki and the owner of West Ham United FC. At the start of 2008, Björgólfur was a billionaire. By the end of that same year, his net worth was reduced to zero. And if we travel in time, we come across countless brilliant individuals and historical icons, including Mark Twain,* Ulysses S. Grant,† and Isaac Newton,‡ who made remarkably foolish investment decisions.

While we are all too aware of irresponsible celebrities, such as Nicolas Cage ($150 million fortune, gone!), entertainers, such as MC Hammer ($33 million fortune, gone!), athletes,[5] such as Mike Tyson ($350 million fortune, gone!) or Curt Shilling ($50 million fortune, gone!), and most lottery winners (multimillion-dollar winners often lose all their winnings within a few short years or even end up poorer than before their win[6]), it is perplexing how capable, smart, and suc-cessful entrepreneurs who have years of experience making good busi-ness decisions could make such poor investment decisions.

Throughout this book, I make the argument that these individ-uals made the mistake of assuming that because they were so capable

---

*Mark Twain filed for bankruptcy after pouring the majority of his family's savings, about $6 million in today's dollars, into a failed start-up (i.e., a mechanical typeset-ter). This experience inspired his famous quote: "There are two times in a man's life when he should not speculate: when he can't afford it, and when he can."
† After completing his second term as president, Grant invested his life savings with Ferdinand Ward, in what proved to be a Ponzi scheme. Grant was left penniless. In an ironic twist of fate, when Grant was dying of cancer, he commissioned his friend Mark Twain to write his life memoirs, hoping to leave his family with a modest inher-itance. Grant completed the memoir on July 18, 1885, five days before he died.
‡ The full story is referenced on page 51.

at creating wealth, they were equally qualified to preserve it. The reality is that the science of *getting rich* is profoundly different from the science of *staying rich*.

There are many fundamental differences between those in the business of wealth creation and those in the business of wealth preservation. One of the key differences is characterized by the types of risk they are willing to undertake. Unlike those who are trying to get rich, those who are trying to stay rich must—at all costs—avoid the risk of permanently losing capital or simply not having the money they need when they need it.

In wealth creation, you have to take big bets and sometimes aim for the fences, knowing that if you strike out you will have other at-bats to make up for it. In wealth preservation, you are keenly aware that your home run attempts are behind you. Now you simply want consistent base hits to stay in the game. But this still means activity. This is active wealth stewardship, not merely wealth ownership. It is remarkable how many investors underestimate the difficulty of simply holding on to their wealth and how much thoughtfulness it requires. To emphasize this point, one of history's savviest financiers, Nathan Mayer Rothschild, once commented, "It requires a great deal of boldness and a great deal of caution to make a great fortune, and when you have got it, it requires ten times as much wit to keep it." As few of us have quite as much wit, we have to hire outside consultants and advisors to ensure that we do not make the mistakes of all those who came before us.

The Industry

There are an estimated 350,000 financial advisors in North America. Almost everyone you know will have one. This is, in fact, a very positive phenomenon with many benefits. Ipsos Reid's 2010 Canadian Financial Monitoring study demonstrated that advised investors are more confident about their future than the non-advised. They also prove to be more comfortable, optimistic, and have better financial prospects than non-advised clients.

Research suggests that investors using advisors are much less likely to be the targets of fraud than those who do not use advisors.[7] With a proper advisor, investors will also mitigate making impetuous, emotional decisions. As Benjamin Graham, the father of value investing, once said, "The investor's chief problem—and even his worst enemy—is likely to be himself."

As a consequence of all these (and other) positive aspects of getting investment advice, advised households have anywhere from three to five times the level of investable assets as non-advised households.[8]

The Challenge

While the benefits are wonderful, the real question is, who can take you to the promised land of better investment decisions and help you meet your financial goals? This may seem like a rather simple question, but it is actually more complex than it sounds. As we will soon see, searching for a true investment advisor may be like looking for a needle in a haystack. Let us begin by understanding the challenges involved.

Semantic Confusion

On July 3, 2013, the Egyptian military overthrew the Islamist-run government of Mohamed Morsi. For months, the United States debated whether to term it a coup or a revolution. What hung in the balance of those two words was $1.5 billion in aid, which Egypt would lose if the US government labeled it a coup. This is an extreme example of how important it is that all parties correctly understand the terminology at work, but the basis of all communication is a shared understanding of meaning. Unfortunately, financial services has many terms, such as *risk*, *return*, and *diversification* that are thrown around casually, and investors' understanding of them is extremely subjective and often quite poor. And it is *advisor*, a term that is most vital to comprehend, that proves to be the most misunderstood term in the financial lexicon. Failure to engage proper investment counsel won't only be costly but may even be catastrophic.

Wikipedia unabashedly points out that "according to the U.S. Financial Industry Regulatory Authority (FINRA), terms such as *financial advisor* and *financial planner* are general terms or job titles used by investment professionals and do not denote any specific designations."[9] FINRA describes the main groups of investment professionals who may use the term *financial advisor* to be "brokers, investment advisors, money managers, accountants, lawyers, insurance agents and financial planners."[10]

To make sure this is truly etched into your mind, it is worth repeating again. Anyone, and I mean anyone, can put up the financial advisor shingle. As Wikipedia notes, "There is little regulatory control exercised over use of the term and, as such, many insurance brokers, insurance agents, securities brokers, financial planners and others identify themselves as financial advisors."[11]

Even if there were no regulations around the term, one would think that paying someone for his or her advice would imply that the person has the qualifications to give advice on the subject (and the ability to put clients' interests ahead of their own). Just as we would expect a physician to have a medical degree, an accountant to have a professional designation, and a lawyer to have passed the bar exam, the term *advisor* evokes for us the suggestion of pedigree, experience, deep education, and sophistication in investing. But this is not the case. Comparing the barriers of entry into financial advisory work to the barriers of entry into other professional services is particularly striking. At one end of the spectrum, there are professionals, such as doctors, lawyers, and accountants, who spend years being educated, complete rigorous examinations, and are monitored by a professional body. At the other end of the spectrum, there are self-declared advisors who don't even need a high-school education, have to pass few or no exams, and are completely unregulated. To sell mutual funds in Canada, for example, one need only pay $375, take the Canadian Investment Funds Course,[12] which is a short online course, and print up some business cards. Outside of this one, specific course, there are *zero* criteria for becoming an investment or financial advisor.*

There are, of course, several respectable designations one has the option of acquiring (e.g., Chartered Financial Analyst or Certified Financial Planner), and there are some knowledgeable and successful advisors who don't have an extensive education. But it's important to understand that competence is not a given. In fact, it is entirely optional.

Wall Street and Bay Street have addressed this lack of regulation and qualification by developing facades of pedigree to address confidence gaps. According to the *Wall Street Journal*, there are anywhere from 150 to 200 different designations for financial advisors.[13] Many of them are basically worthless, requiring nothing more than a weekend course or an open-book exam online, allowing one to slap a few ambiguous letters after his or her name. To further provide an air of sophistication, firms selling financial products will generally hire very affable individuals with dynamic personalities (and fast-talking often seems to be part of the job description). To add a bit more gravitas, these firms often hire mature individuals a few decades into their careers to provide the illusion of experience and the ability to advise.

All this is problematic because research suggests that the masses are actually relying on their advisors for advice, which—given the low barriers of entry—they may not be qualified to provide. Various studies suggest that 71 percent of investors over the age of thirty-five use

---

* In some Canadian jurisdictions there are some title limitations and even proposals to introduce title reform, limiting who can refer to themselves as advisors. Though, at the time of this printing, it is far from obvious to the consumer who is actually offering them advice and who is simply attempting to sell financial product.

an advisor to learn about financial information,[14] and 55 percent of all investors cite an advisor as their most referenced source for information about investing.[15] In fact, almost all study respondents, approximately 91 percent, considered an advisor to be one of the primary sources for help with investment decisions.[16] Considering the trust vested in the knowledge and expertise of financial advisors, one would hope that it is warranted. Yet, given the low level of requirements for putting up that shingle, true knowledge and expertise is far from assured.

To be fair, you don't need any designation or pedigree to be a great advisor. Take, for example, the famous story of investor Todd Combs. Combs heard Warren Buffett speak at Columbia Business School. One of Combs's classmates asked Buffett what his advice would be to young people interested in making a career out of investing. Buffett responded by reaching to his right and picking up a stack of financial reports and papers he had brought with him, saying, "Read five hundred pages like this every day."

Todd Combs, unlike most of his Columbia classmates, took Buffett's words to heart. He started reading voraciously, eventually surpassing five hundred pages of reading every day. After successfully running an investment partnership for many years, Combs eventually returned to Buffett and had a conversation with him. The conversation developed into a meeting, which developed into a job interview. Today, Todd Combs manages over $5 billion of Berkshire Hathaway's investments. He, along with another portfolio manager, is expected to succeed Warren Buffett as a chief investment officer at the behemoth investing company. And he maintains his reading regimen to this day.

Any advisor, regardless of background, can, theoretically, fall into this category—though the data suggests that, regrettably, Todd Combs is by far the exception, not the rule.

Culture of Salesmanship or Culture of Stewardship

Another major (and perhaps the most significant) challenge in the industry is compensation alignment. Unlike other professional practitioners who are paid for their time and/or services provided, many financial advisors are paid based on trading fees, a percentage of assets, some form of commission, or a combination of all three. A flat retainer model or an hourly fee arrangement does exist, but it is still a rare breed in the industry.

The combination of the scarcity of true investment expertise and the asset acquisition or sales compensation model has had a severe impact on the culture of the industry as a whole. As opposed to a culture of stewardship, it has become a culture of salesmanship. Financial advisors should concern themselves with prudence, cost consciousness, and caution, but compensation models motivate the exact opposite behaviors. In fact, the irony of financial products is that commissions are usually lower for safer, fixed-income vehicles than they are for complex, high-risk vehicles. This means that not only is fiscal prudence muddled but risk levels may be improperly incentivized.

Imagine if your doctor was compensated based on the medicines you purchased or how often you changed medications. Or imagine if your lawyer was compensated based on the lawsuits you engaged in. This compensation model can only create toxic dynamics, and in the world of financial advisors, it incentivizes handing money to the advisor or buying investment products. It's hard to see how any advice offered under such a model could be valuable.

That is precisely why Warren Buffett has often criticized the practice of labeling brokers as investment advisors. Buffett has said this misnomer is akin to calling a car salesman a transportation advisor or calling a grocery store clerk a nutritional advisor. He points out that the distinction between brokers and advisors is supposed to be similar to the distinction between pharmacists and doctors. One fills the prescriptions, but it is the other who diagnoses and prescribes the medicine.

Finance = Distribution

A friend of mine, who is a veteran of the financial service industry and founder of several wealth management institutions, frequently lectures at a prominent Canadian business school. At the start of his seminars, he would often approach the long wraparound blackboard in the lecture hall and offer the following prompt to the class: "Imagine this board is the universe of financial service jobs available to you. How much of this blackboard represents jobs in product development, research, or asset management, and how much of it represents sales and distribution?" The students would usually agree that the majority of the blackboard belonged in the former and a tiny sliver of the blackboard belonged in the latter. My friend would then provide these enthusiastic graduate students with their first dose of reality: "Ninety percent of you are thinking that you will end up in corporate finance, financial analysis and money management because that is where the interesting jobs are. But if current numbers in the industry are indicative of future numbers, over 90 percent of you will end up in sales and distribution."

This focus on distribution has pushed the popularity of many new financial products and services. For example, nearly 50 percent of all mutual fund assets under management today are held in wrap accounts or funds of funds. These are appealing to financial institutions because they eliminate most of the heavy lifting associated with investing, allowing them to collect trailers for simply redistributing, and adding little to no value along the way. The problems with this model for retail investors are numerous. Their investment decisions are made in a vacuum, with no consideration for asset allocation, alternatives, rebalancing, due diligence, or meeting long-term financial goals. On top of this, at a certain point, the numerous added layers of fees make outperformance highly unlikely, if not almost statistically impossible. Sadly, these funds of funds and wrapped vehicles are actually becoming more popular with unsophisticated investors, not less so.[17]

Even regulated fiduciaries, which are much more constrained, do not look at the sales side of the equation. Those working in sales are mandated to make only "suitable" recommendations. This is a deliberately vague standard with highly flexible ethics around the word *suitable*. In this culture of salesmanship, it becomes very difficult for advisors to put the clients' interests ahead of their own. While most financial advisors are good, hardworking people who sincerely care about their clients and the people around them, always acting in the best interests of those clients becomes much more difficult when one's financial incentives are poorly aligned with (and sometimes diametrically opposed to) the clients'.

In the spring of 1997, noted author and journalist Jason Zweig was invited to speak to fund executives at a dinner held in conjunction with the annual meeting of the Investment Company Institute. At that occasion, Jason boldly admonished those in the room who were in the "marketing business" rather than in the "investment business." By that, he meant that those who claimed they were advisors were in effect glorified salesmen. He criticized the firms that clandestinely and simultaneously incubate many new funds and then promote the hell out of those that do well and covertly kill those that do not. He railed against the practice of continuing to promote funds without prospect for success, of incentivizing portfolio managers to grow their asset base instead of their performance, of failing to educate clients, and of charging fees that are not commensurate with the value being offered. The audience was so infuriated by Zweig's remarks that attendees stood up and proceeded to scream at him during his presentation.

Zweig has been among a handful of investor activists who are trying to drive home the message—to both investors and investment professionals alike—that there is unquestionably much money to be made selling financial products, but that is a far cry from advice, selling strategy, or expertise.*

Disclosure and Transparency of Financial Advice

How often do we hear of a skyscraper falling down because the foundation of the building was overstressed or because the edifice was used for more taxing purposes than was intended? I never have. Yet, in just the last few years, financial skyscrapers like Lehman Brothers and Bear Stearns have collapsed from the weight of greed and excessive leverage although they were financially engineered by some of the brightest minds in America.

This level of complexity in financial products creates a need for transparency—especially when it comes to compensation and the alignment of interests. However, advisors are under no obligation to disclose all the ways that they are paid and incentivized.† And even well-intentioned advisors don't want to disclose anything that could be perceived as a weakness. If the advisors fully disclosed all the fees they charge, what returns they would have to generate to justify those fees, and how far down the totem pole retail investors are placed, their weakness would show (and investors would be aghast). Not only do regulations shelter advisors from revealing their weakness but the investors serve as unwitting accomplices to the industry's obscurity. Investors often don't know the right questions to ask and what is considered to be an appropriate or

---

* Incidentally, a strong sales culture often connotes weak returns. Some of the most accomplished investors and managers we've interacted with do not want to grow their asset base, they are not interested in entertaining clients, and they will not budge on their principals. These individuals can charge the higher fees, impose stricter liquidity terms, require higher minimum investments, and dictate how often they will communicate with clients. Their long-term performance does all the selling they need.
† Though, there is now a strong move afoot by regulators in most developed markets to change that. In Canada, we recently saw the arrival of Client Relationship Model, Phase 2 (CRM2), which now requires investment advisors to be more transparent about how they have performed and how much they actually charge by listing specific fees and providing an aggregate dollar figure for each twelve-month period.

inappropriate response. After all, that is what they have an advisor for. A good advisor helps an investor ask the right questions, ensure all concerns are properly addressed, and everyone involved (themselves included) is held to account. But how do you know you have a good advisor?

Service Limitations

Besides the inability to offer clarity on the inner architecture of financial services, many advisors do not bother consulting on the key areas of a client's finances, such as cash-flow management, budgeting, tax, philanthropy, and retirement and estate planning. These are not high-priority items for most advisors, as they rarely allow for the chance to sell you something, yielding minimal to no compensation for them. Just imagine the likelihood of an advisor recommending that you sell the funds you hold to pay down some debt or to buy a superior investment through another advisor or to diversify away from the financial product(s) he or she is representing. Some advisors will certainly want to help with some strategic and planning aspects, but this assistance is little more than goodwill—akin to their desire to recommend a good Italian restaurant—as opposed to being a professional endeavor.

There is a sad local story that punctuates this reality, told by Alan Goldhar, who is a professor of financial planning at York University and who has served in a leadership role as an Ontario public trustee. The Office of the Public Guardian and Trustee is charged with taking control of finances for individuals in the Province of Ontario who have died without a will or are mentally unstable and cannot make responsible financial decisions. In recent years, advisors have taken over $500 million in investments from more than ten thousand clients.[18] Virtually all these individuals had a financial advisor or a broker, and yet not a single one of these individuals had a financial plan.[19] How mortifying it is to think that these people had advisors who were only too happy to profit off their backs without a single advisor ensuring his or her clients' needs were being met and interests protected.

Product, Platform, and Philosophy Constraints

Although we have looked at shortcomings in advisors in terms of their own moral compass and desire to excel in their profession, it should be noted that they are often constrained by the firm sponsoring their license. Most financial advisors are significantly limited in which investment options they can offer their clients. For example, if they are part of a private wealth group in a bank, they may be constrained by products offered by the bank's asset management group.* And even if advisors are independent of a large financial institution, they may only offer financial products that are created in-house or may only build portfolios made up of just a few asset classes (e.g., stocks, bonds, options, and cash.). In both these cases, poor diversification is virtually guaranteed because the menu of options is limited.

Whether it is the proprietary funds of the financial institution they are associated with or simply the structural or regulatory limitations they have, most advisors' product offerings are remarkably narrow. They are driven by convenience, scalability, profit margins, and ease of accessibility rather than by the needs and aspirations of the client.

When incentivizing advisors with either percentage-of-assets or transaction-based compensation, the drive toward efficiency and scale will invariably limit the type of asset classes or the types of investment

---

* In the summer of 2012, there was a disturbing story that three of Morningstar's top-performing fund sponsors—Leith Wheeler, Mawer, and Steadyhand—were cut from RBC's discount brokerage, RBC Direct Investing. While RBC described the move as simply a business decision, many in the investment community claimed this was due to the fact that the funds offered by these firms do not pay trailers and thus were not as profitable for RBC.

opportunities an advisor will participate in. Public equities and bonds are an obvious default. In the public markets, advisors can load up on almost as much or as little of an opportunity as they like. In contrast, for most advisors, direct participation in real estate, infrastructure, private equity, and a number of other asset classes is inefficient because they are difficult to access, tedious to conduct proper due diligence on, and unscalable. It is obviously easier for the advisor and more profitable for the institution to avoid these asset classes, but this may not be optimal for an investor whose circumstances may require exposure to them.

The Silver Bullet Narrative

The only thing worse than an advisor with limited options is one who believes those are all the options anyone needs. Even legendary investment manager Ray Dalio developed the All Weather and the All Seasons portfolios, which claimed to be resilient and profitable in all market environments. Similarly, in his most recent book, *Money: Master the Game*, motivational speaker Tony Robbins naively touts this portfolio as the "ideal portfolio." While Ray Dalio has certainly proven himself to be an extraordinary investor for a number of reasons,* it is doubtful that the success of this portfolio will be replicated in the decades ahead.

The reality is there is no single narrative in finance. There is no single strategy, asset class, or even investment philosophy that works at all times and in all seasons. That is precisely why in 2013 the Royal Swedish Academy of Sciences selected two economists—Eugene Fama and Robert Shiller—with diametrically opposed, even contradictory,

---

* Besides the Bridgewater's recent struggles, what is most disconcerting is that Dalio's portfolio has a high allocation to bonds (55 percent of the portfolio). Given that interest rates are at all-time lows and could only go up, portfolio returns will invariably be dampened, as bonds and interest rates are inversely correlated (i.e., when rates go up, bonds go down).

views as winners of the Nobel Prize in Economics.* The reality is that both are right, just at different times.[20] That is also the reason John Bogle, the granddaddy of index investing, the most vocal advocate of passive investing, and the legendary founder of the Vanguard Group, still invests in active-managed mutual funds. Not everything is as clear cut as some advisors make it out to be.[21] As anyone who is biblically literate can attest, *there is a time for everything, and a season for every activity under the heavens.*[22]

So how can investors avoid the risk of being cornered into a particular product or limited in the asset classes they can invest in? Unfortunately, the answer to that is nothing short of an unbiased investment consultant or advisor who has no proprietary products to sell and is not compensated by the assets he or she gathers.

Conflicts of Interest

Kent Womack's study of the buy and sell recommendations of fourteen major US brokerage firms with investment advisory practices found that buy recommendations occurred seven times more often than sell recommendations.[23] These findings raise the question of how it is possible that brokerage firms, whose job is to provide equally recommendations when to buy and when to sell, seem to be providing only half the service. The answer is driven by conflicts of interest.

There are many potential sources of conflicts of interest in financial services. It has even been said that "conflicts of interest aren't a part of how Wall Street does business; conflicts are its stock-in-trade."[24] This is especially disconcerting with conflicts that are not readily apparent. For example, conflicts are heightened when the different arms of a financial conglomerate operate under a single umbrella brand. In such a scenario, in order for the investment banking arm to get the underwriting

---

* More formally known as the Sveriges Riksbank Prize in Economic Sciences in Memory of Alfred Nobel.

business the investment bank may leverage the fact that the asset management arm holds a large stake in the company. Conversely, a large-scale deal on the investment banking side with a particular company may present a conflict to the asset manager who wants to sell off their significant holding in the same company. Accordingly, sell recommendations have the potential to hurt a brokerage firm's investment banking relationships and limit the flow of information to its analysts; and that's beside the fact that the fees are usually lower on the sale than on the purchase of securities for a client.

A trustworthy advisor, then, must be unmoved by the needs and demands of marketers, salespeople, and even his or her own CEO. A trustworthy advisor must not be influenced by any other outcome other than what is in the best interest of the client.*

It is astounding that the concept of a trustworthy advisor is still novel in financial services. By definition, an advisor is selling his expertise, not any particular product. Having any financial allegiance or relationship with a particular product or service should immediately tarnish the qualification of an advisor, and yet it is perfectly acceptable. Who would give any credence to a restaurant critic that is employed by TGI Friday's or a car consultant who owns a Honda dealership? Yet the field of financial services is teeming with these sorts of conflicts of interest.

Not surprisingly, studies at the Harvard Business School have shown that buying from those who are compensated by the products they sell actually translates into poor performance. These products tend to underperform funds that are bought directly by the investor, even before deducting the additional fees related to the compensation of the advisor. What buying from these individuals will achieve is

---

* That is why in the United States all Registered Investment Advisors are actually regulated fiduciaries where they are legally required to put the interests of their clients ahead of their own. Shockingly, in Canada, IIROC- or MFDA-certified advisors are not. Most Canadian investors are not aware of this and, perhaps worse, don't understand the implications.

more trend chasing and succumbing to behavioral biases, along with a higher likelihood of buying funds that are front-loaded (i.e., you pay upfront fees for buying them). [25]

A study on German investors has shown that commission-compensated advisors create many problems for investors. Their advice increased portfolio risk and increased the probabilities of losses, which increased trading frequency and portfolio turnover, when compared to what investors would do on their own.[26] This problem is only further exacerbated by the fact that, according to research published by the National Bureau of Economic Research, investors tend to consult with product-oriented financial advisors before purchasing investments. Investors do this to manage their own biases, but they are actually adding fuel to the fire they are trying to prevent.[27] This is why Warren Buffett has repeatedly cautioned, "Never ask a barber if you need a haircut."

Those advisors who work for a publicly traded financial company have the added pressure of constantly up-selling, cross-selling, and widening margins in order for their firms to increase earnings and share price, which may be where they hold most of their options and stock.

It is worth noting that just because someone is conflicted does not automatically invalidate the investment. It simply suggests that there may be other agendas to consider, and one must ensure that the investment opportunities are compelling notwithstanding those agendas.

Similarly, we should bear in mind that those who have conflicts are not unethical individuals. Most people are not even cognizant of all the conflicts that riddle their professional lives. A recent study demonstrated that people are quite good at identifying conflicts of interest in other professions but poor at identifying those in their own.[28] In this study, several hundred physicians and an equivalent number of financial planners were asked to evaluate conflict-of-interest policies. One half of the physicians had to evaluate policies for medical professionals and one half of the physicians had to evaluate policies for financial professionals. The financial planners were also split in half and given the same task. In their assessments, the physicians were incensed by the notion that financial professionals might receive gifts (e.g., mugs, pens, lunches) from investment companies (i.e., of financial products). But they totally dismissed the idea that if physicians received the same treatment from drug companies it would ever compromise their integrity. Likewise, financial planners had zero tolerance for medical professionals accepting gifts from pharmaceutical companies, but felt that similar constraints in financial services were needless and excessive.

The bottom line is that people have a bias blind spot.[29] They are good at spotting the potential ulterior motives of others but quite poor at recognizing what may cloud their own objectivity. The takeaway for investors is to ascertain what conflicts play a role with your prospective advisor before hiring him or her. Once you have identified any existing conflicts, assuming you continue using their services, ensure that your interests are never compromised as a result.

It may go without saying, but simply lacking conflicts of interest does not make anyone's advice wise or worthwhile. It is remarkable how many people consult with family members and friends on financial matters in which neither has any expertise. The key here is to find experts who have the fewest possible conflicts, who share your values, and who have as much investment knowledge as possible.

Prescriptive, Not Predictive, Advice

While expertise is critical in investing, one would be best served by avoiding experts who exude certainty about tomorrow. Such certainty is either couched in self-serving commercial interest or is just a symptom of foolhardiness.

Those involved in the manufacturing or distribution of a particular investment strategy will not attempt to put themselves out of a job. They will mold their investment philosophy around their own asset class or strategy and stand ready to tell a story aligned with their vocation. Which bond manager will tell you bonds are now the riskiest investment? Which emerging market equity manager will tell you to put the brakes on? Regardless of what the markets are doing, if their jobs depend on it, these managers are likely to defend their relevance and confidence in every situation.

At the turn of this century, billions of dollars were being poured into the tech sector in every corner of the developed world with the attitude that this is *definitely* a new world, a new economy where earnings are irrelevant. Technology funds were opening up everywhere in response to this certainty. But this arrogance at the top levels is no different from the CNBC-type assertions that tell you every day where the market is *definitely* going and giving grossly oversimplified reasons why it's going there.

The problem, of course, lies in the fact that conviction sells. Jason Zweig has written about our biological tendency to forecast the future even when we know it's unpredictable, and to identify patterns pointing to the future even when we know it is random.* He calls this our "prediction addiction." Humans have a need for certainty and gravitate toward it despite all the evidence against it.[30] People will always prefer something neatly packaged, simple, and predictable, over something complex, messy, and random. So when a money manager, a broker, or an advisor offers certainty, it is hard not to believe in it.†

---

* Since time immemorial, members of the media have been making dramatic, strident, and wildly inaccurate predictions about the future. For example, in 1894, prominent British newspapers predicted that with the alarming growth of horse-drawn carriages, by 1944 the streets of London would be buried under nine feet of manure.

† The irony is that I frequently encounter advisors or managers with some of the most compelling investment products and impressive performance records who are among the world's worst salespeople, while I have consistently encountered individuals who have second-rate products and pitiful performance records with powerhouse sales teams or exceptionally convincing marketing arms.

Unfortunately, reality is gray, murky, and uncomfortable. Financial services, markets, and investments are neither simple nor neat. Education and nuance is required, and most investors are simply not up to the challenge.

There is a well-known debate in philosophical circles on predictability. Determinists, like the French astronomer and mathematician Pierre-Simon Laplace, believe that if we had perfect knowledge of present conditions (i.e., understanding every scientific fact and dynamic in the universe), we would have the ability to make perfect predictions.[31] Probabilists, such as Werner Heisenberg, who famously posited the uncertainty principle, believe that even with perfect knowledge, conditions are eternally uncertain. Not only will conditions in the future be uncertain but even the state of today's affairs is ambiguous, making predictions about our world murky at best.

Heisenberg has been proven correct over and over, as even with the advent of countless technologies that have put infinitely more information at our fingertips, we have become no better at economic predictions, but Wall Street still holds strong to its determinist beliefs. There are those that sell the message that not only do we perfectly understand what is happening today but we are also pretty damn confident about what it will mean for the future. Whether it's on Bloomberg, CNBC, BNN (in Canada), or any other channel that propagates market predictions, there is no shortage of investment gurus and economists confidently explaining the market to us.

The reality is that these opinions are most often useless and often detrimental to investors. In fact, when finance academics John Graham and Campbell Harvey studied stock-predicting newsletters, they came to two conclusions. First, results of these prediction newsletters were so atrocious that they questioned whether the predictions were arrived at by chance. And second, they found that one would be more successful finding the worst of the newsletters and doing the opposite of what they recommended.[32] It is not what anyone wants to hear, but the truth is that the world is far more complex and unpredictable than a newsletter, an algorithm, or a cable news show would have us believe.

Not only is the market as a whole unpredictable but even individual securities are fairly erratic in the short term. In one study, a few dozen undergraduate students from the Stockholm School of Economics were matched up with a few dozen stock market analysts. All of them were asked to analyze the twenty-eight stocks listed on the Stockholm Stock Exchange and forecast their prices three months out.* Amazingly, the stock market professionals actually made less-accurate predictions than the undergraduate students.[33]

There is no shortage of similar stories, whether it is the one about the Playboy models whose stock picks outperformed most mutual fund managers,[34] or the one where Orlando the cat defeated three money manager opponents in a stock market challenge,[35] or the one of Burton Malkiel's one hundred blindfolded monkeys that outperformed the index.[36] Stock market forecasters are unreliable in the short run, and analysts tend to be fairly poor prophets. Perhaps that is why Mark Twain was once quoted as saying, "The best way to make money from stocks is to sell investment advice."[37]

Notably, economic prognosticators have an even more dismal record, and unlike talented stock pickers, they can be wrong for a very long time. In one study, the leading financial executives in the United States were asked to predict one-year and ten-year stock market returns along with the best-case and worst-case scenarios for the market. Over 11,600 forecasts from experts were submitted for the prospects of the S&P 500. One would presume that the accumulated sophistication of these market leaders, along with their many years of experience, would provide them with some insight. When the data was tabulated, however, not only was there no positive correlation

---

* The absurdity of this exercise is the time horizon involved. While successful security selection is possible over an investment cycle, within the short-term anything is possible. As Benjamin Graham once said, "In the short run, the market is a voting machine but in the long run, it is a weighing machine." .

between the predictions of these financial experts and the value of the S&P 500, there was actually a negative one.[38] A similar result emerged in the United Kingdom, where the ten-year economic predictions of former ministers of finance were pitted against the predictions of London dustmen. The dustmen proved much more prescient than their more illustrious counterparts.[39] In each of these cases, the experts actually proved to be better at predicting the exact opposite of what would unfold.

There is only one thing worse than experts acting as prophets, which is experts acting as prophets with the cameras rolling. Philip Tetlock, professor of psychology and management at the University of Pennsylvania, has spent the last thirty years studying experts and their ability to make sound predictions. He published a masterful work on the subject, *Expert Political Judgment: How Good Is It? How Can We Know?* His research suggests that there is almost no domain where experts can demonstrate better predictive power than nonexperts with a calculator and an understanding of the historic base-rate. More experience, higher IQs, and even being more educated did not provide a greater capacity to make predictions about the future. There was, however, one trait that proved to be highly correlated with predictive capacity: media attention. Unfortunately, it was inversely correlated. As he writes, "experts who made more media appearances tended to be worse predictors."[40] In fact, not only did those with the most exposure have the least accurate forecasts, but those who received the most publicity proved to have the poorest results even after long periods of outperformance.

In a similar vein of research, a study from the University of Richmond looked at all the cover stories that adorned *Business Week*, *Forbes*, and *Fortune* over a twenty-year period. They categorized all the covers by whether the editorial was bullish or bearish about the featured companies. Each of the companies that were in the bullish category had outperformed by an average of 42 percent over the prior two years. Each of the companies that the magazines were bearish about had underperformed by an average of 35 percent over the prior two years. However, in the two years after their cover stories, the stocks of the bearish companies—who were criticized—outperformed the bullish companies—who were applauded—by a factor of almost three to one.[41]

In case you thought this was a function of outdated technology and that the experts of yesteryear were simply not as sophisticated as the experts of today, think again. Data suggests that our experts are actually becoming duller. In a study conducted by David Dreman and Michael Berry, comparing 66,100 financial analyst estimates with actual results, it was discovered that the gap between estimates and results grew over time.[42] In other words, despite finance becoming more technically sophisticated, the analysis (as defined by its predictive ability) is actually getting worse.[43]

The reality is that the best investors are only one-eyed kings in the land of the blind. An analyst may be 100 percent right about the facts underpinning an investment and simultaneously be 100 percent wrong about the investment itself. The best investors, then, acknowledge that they are constantly making decisions with imperfect information. As J. P. Morgan, after being asked what the market will do next, once wisely remarked, "It will fluctuate."

Final Thoughts on Financial Advisors

The term *financial advisor* is deceiving and makes finding good investment advice an arduous task. To be clear, there is a place in the market for brokers, bankers, investment managers, and financial advisors. Each of these has a role to play in any healthy marketplace. Consumers should just know which ones they are hiring and the costs associated with their services.

In order to make good decisions, investment advisors who sell investments and are compensated by the volume of sales should be correctly addressed as financial salespeople and not as advisors.* To describe these salespeople as offering financial advisory services is akin to describing used-car dealerships as providing transportation consulting services. Used-car dealerships and salespeople serve an important role in our economy, but their jobs aren't to serve as auto advisors; they are to sell cars. In the same vein, most of the investment advisors that sell investments and are compensated by the volume of sales should be correctly addressed as financial salespeople—not as advisors. There is nothing unsavory about sales or salespeople. These tireless individuals drive the engine of our economy and are critical to any company's success. But there is no denying their roles and their motivations, and there is something unsavory about thinking you're paying for advice when you are paying for product.

These are not just semantics or technicalities. These misnomers can carry a very long list of consequences. In Germany, for example, nearly 80 percent of long-term investments are terminated prematurely because of poor and unsuitable financial advice.[44] In other words, investors were sold instead of advised, and when they realized it, they ran for the exit. The financial impact of this advice deficiency is estimated to cost German investors as much as €30 billion each year.[45]

Fortunately, the landscape is starting to shift. Through the proliferation of information and online resources, consumers are becoming more educated. Even the masses have picked up on the fact that there are major concerns with financial services and that the advice they receive is profoundly inadequate. According to the 2012 Edelman Public Policy Report, which surveyed more than thirty-one thousand people in twenty-six countries† and measured the level of trust within industries, financial services and banks have been the two least trusted industries for the past three years.[46]

---

* In the 1980s, IDA registrants were called "stock brokers" because they brokered stocks. Today, they continue to broker stocks, but with the fancy and deceptive new title of *advisor*.
† Survey was conducted with members of the "informed public" (i.e., college graduates whose household income is in the top quartile for their age in their country and who follow public-policy issues in the news at least several times a week).

This is especially notable when one compares these results to the automotive industry, where even with all its aggressive sales practices it is still 22 percent more trusted than financial institutions in the United States and around the world.[47]

In part due to these frustrations, very affluent families have tried to remove themselves from the market and create their own in-house solutions, commonly referring to them as the *family office*. If properly done, the family office may be the best model to professionally manage one's wealth. Fully staffed, this would include a chief investment officer and a chief financial officer, as well as a professional research team and back-office personnel. Having these unbiased professionals on your team would be invaluable and would support best-practice investing. However, it would cost. If, on top of the personnel, you include the costs of facilities, technology, and supplies, the overhead on the operation could easily exceed $1 million per year.* To warrant such an operation would require at least $100 million in investable assets. Some even argue that investing in and managing a proper family office with less than $500 million is imprudent.[48]

For most investors, a proper family office is too costly, and for those who could afford it, they may not want the hassle of setting up and managing such an infrastructure. So where does this leave most investors? What other options and resources are available to them? Or is the best option to forget about getting outside help and just forge alone, figuring it out as they go?

These are the questions we will deal with in the sections ahead.

---

* This is assuming a $400,000-plus salary for a seasoned CIO and a $250,000-plus salary for a seasoned CFO, with an additional $350,000 to cover the research and back-office team.

KEY TAKEAWAYS FROM PART I

- The science of staying rich is different than the science of getting rich.
- Good investment advice is invaluable, but there is confusion in the industry about who is capable of offering it.
- To identify your best advisor, you need to distinguish between salesmen and stewards—between those who have conflicts of interest and those who are squarely in your corner.
- Proper investment advice is prescriptive not predictive. It will not claim to be able to forecast the future state of markets.

PART II

THE INVESTOR

The first principle is that you must not fool yourself—
and you are the easiest person to fool.

—Richard Feynman

The difficulty with best-practice investing is that it is somewhat unnatural and at times counterintuitive for successful individuals who have spent their energy creating meaningful wealth. To counteract the challenge of switching gears from creating to investing wealth, there are four key elements that every investor must ensure he or she is adhering to. These include adopting greater humility, getting (re)educated, creating conditions for investing with independence, and hiring proper investment counsel. We will explore each of these in the pages ahead.

Humility

Perhaps the most difficult element that successful entrepreneurs-turned-investors have to be mindful of is humility. To have achieved a degree of success that will allow you to retire and live off your wealth is an exceptional feat. Most launched businesses prove to be unsuccessful, and of those that are profitable, fewer still translate into a liquidity event that creates meaningful wealth. After achieving this exceptional creation of wealth, then, it is difficult to accept that having success in creating wealth does not necessarily mean having success in preserving wealth. This requires tremendous humility, and humility is not an easy lesson given that even less successful creators of wealth consider themselves above-average investors.

Study after study has shown that people tend to regard themselves as being above average. Whether it comes to attractiveness, driving ability, likelihood of being divorced, or even getting suckered into a bad deal, most people consider themselves above average.[1] They assume they are better looking, better drivers,[2] better spouses, better shoppers, and less likely to be defrauded than the average joe—and sometimes by a wide margin.[3] Of course, for the majority to be above average is statistically impossible,* but we believe it, and this tendency is even more pronounced with investors.† Jason Zweig highlights a fascinating study where more than 74 percent of investors fully expected their own funds would beat the S&P 500 every single year.[4] As the expression goes, "The market is a weird place. Every time one guy sells, another one buys, and they both think they're smart." It is exceedingly difficult for investors to admit their limitations, and even more difficult to find the humility to do something about their limitations.

Being honest with yourself and finding a healthy dose of humility is a requirement for good investing decisions. Some of the most successful investors in the world are renowned for their humility and their ability to keep themselves honest, regardless of which decisions they made or which courses of action they followed. Indeed, humility allows both the investor and the advisor to recognize that they could have misread the opportunity or situation and to cut themselves loose to live another day.

---

* In referencing these studies, Berkley professor Terry Odean shared a comical anecdote: "A couple of years ago, one student rated herself below average, and I had to ask her why. She said that she was going to put herself in the top quartile, but then she realized that in the last year she had been in three accidents, had received two speeding tickets, and was going to court to try to prevent her license from being suspended. With all of this evidence, it occurred to her that perhaps she was only about average. Only once have I ever had someone rate himself in the bottom 10 percent of drivers. I was shocked when it happened. When I asked him why, he answered that he did not drive because he was from a foreign country."

† According to Boston-based investment-research firm Dalbar Inc., in the twenty years through 2011, the S&P 500 index generated an annualized return of 7.8 percent, but the average investor achieved an annualized return of only 3.5 percent. For bond investors, when compared to the Barclays Capital Aggregate Bond Index, the results were even more abysmal.

On the infamous Black Monday in 1987, George Soros was bleeding badly. He had believed that the Japanese economy was in for a crash and decided to aggressively short Tokyo stocks while buying futures of the S&P in New York. While he was ultimately correct about Japan, on October 19, this strategy was working against him in the worst possible way. The Japanese government was temporarily supporting the market while the Dow had plummeted 22.6 percent in one day. Without batting an eyelash, Soros believed he had misread the opportunity and went on an aggressive sell-off and crystalized his losses.

History has shown that markets don't always recover, and you cannot always hold on to ride the wave back up. Prior to 1914, the Saint Petersburg exchange was one of the most dynamic and respected bond markets in the world. As a result of the havoc wreaked by World War I, the Saint Petersburg bourse shut down and never reopened. This is not a unique story. Political or military upheaval has shut down many other securities or bond markets around the world. Some notable ones include Cairo, Buenos Aires, Shanghai, and Bombay.[5]

George Soros is not a man who is intimidated by the markets. However, when he believes he may have been wrong, conviction will not compromise his humility. Whether they are advisors or investors, those with discipline and a value orientation are not worried about the intraday ups and downs of the market, but they are smart enough to know that if an investment will go to zero, any point at which one exits is better than the alternative. Humility will allow one to catch a mistake early and avoid butchering a portfolio by continuing to stay in a sinking ship. Humility has to be part and parcel of the culture of any investment shop, whether on the advisory side or on the money management side. There are stories about money managers who keep a prominently displayed Wall of Shame in their offices with a list of all their failed investments as a humble reminder of their vulnerability and incentive to avoid similar mistakes in the future.

It is human nature to favor information that supports our views and beliefs. We tend to ignore contradictory evidence or interpret our world in light of what we already know or believe. Those with a proper dose of humility, however, are more introspective, analyzing past mistakes and questioning their own beliefs in the present, making every effort to avoid falling into the trap of a confirmation bias the next time. In some ways, it becomes a perpetual struggle. As George Soros once lamented, "By and large I found managing a hedge fund extremely painful. I could never acknowledge my success, because that might stop me from worrying, but I had no trouble recognizing my mistakes."[6]

There is, of course, a need for some level of confidence. If we truly contemplated every possible way for us to lose money, it is highly likely we would never invest. There is a great deal of uncertainty in everything we do, and investing is, by definition, uncertain. Storing cash under our mattresses is the closest we can come to certainty. Such a tactic, however, may mean that we won't meet our needs or achieve our broader financial goals. So, while it is important for us to recognize our limitations, we must also take risk. And this is where having a trusted, highly competent advisor can help.

(Re)Education

Familiarizing ourselves with all asset classes allows us to properly diversify and avoid overconcentration in any single asset class. However, sometimes after having made one's fortune in one industry or having had a disproportionate number of experiences in one space, there is a tendency to assume that this is the only safe haven for making money. This may be a cousin of the "man-with-a-hammer" syndrome, to whom everything looks like a nail.

Because of what social scientists have referred to as the *confirmation bias*, we gravitate to what we know. In 1965, researcher Timothy Brock showed that when presented with two magazine articles, one with the title "Smoking Does Not Lead to Lung Cancer" and the other "Smoking Leads to Lung Cancer," smokers resoundingly read the first and ignored the second. The same study showed that the converse was true of nonsmokers.[7] Be it in politics, business, or any other realm, countless studies have reached the same conclusion. People tend to pay heed only to those agreeing with them and tend to ignore those that don't. It is, unfortunately, no different in investing, where investors select information and assess risk on the basis of what they have done, experienced, and believed in the past.

Social science and behavioral psychology has demonstrated that our understanding of risk is skewed by what is more vivid than what is more likely. For example, people are much more fearful of tornadoes than they are of asthma because the chaos of a tornado can be vividly imagined while asthma is a quiet image of a person coughing. However, asthma takes many more lives than tornadoes.[8] In the same way, smoking kills many more people than guns, and cars are nearly sixty-five times more likely to kill you than an airplane. Yet people are way more terrified of guns and flying in airplanes than they are of cigarettes and driving cars.

This fear of what is most vividly imagined carried over into investing, where all too often individuals who have created great wealth through *active* involvement in real estate or making widgets think they can meet their financial goals by *passively* investing in the same arenas. These individuals believe that investing in other widget companies is less risky than all their alternatives because the prospect of losing money by investing in unfamiliar assets is a vivid and terrifying image, but slowly running out of money over the long term (which may be more likely) is more difficult to imagine.

Whether or not direct investments into widget companies (i.e., private equity) are safer than other asset classes, the risk barometer of these investors is profoundly mistuned. As a consequence, they are limiting their investment tool kits and may be failing to meet their investment goals.

Studies demonstrate that most investors don't understand basic investment and financial concepts, including diversification, compound interest, risk/return, and securities fraud. Most aren't really aware of investment costs or the impact of those costs on investment returns.[9] That is just one explanation for why so few retain wealth over long periods of time. J.P. Morgan Private Bank conducted a study of all those listed on the Forbes 400 (i.e., America's four hundred wealthiest individuals) between 1982 and 2003. Over those two decades, fewer than 15 percent of these individuals retained their spot on the list. What was most responsible for this erosion of wealth? Overconcentration.[10] Invariably, the job of creating wealth gets confused with the job of preserving it. Investors feel safest within the asset class or the field they know best, but poorly diversified portfolios provide express tickets to the land of wealth reduction.

One of the first challenges of good advisors is to properly educate investors about all asset classes and investment strategies, informing them how to leverage all the options that may be available to them.

Ignorance Is Independent of Risk

Part of getting educated is not writing off particular markets, asset classes, or opportunities solely because you are unfamiliar with them. Familiarity and risk are not correlated, despite the fact that people think they are. Social scientists refer to this as the "mere exposure effect."* One can understand how individuals who have previously made money in real estate or in financing mortgages will tend to believe that the safest way to preserve their wealth is in the same fashion, but even employees of public companies make this mistake.

By having daily exposure to the branding, the facilities, and all the items of their employer, studies have shown that employees tend

---

* This is a cousin of the *home bias*, where we believe native investments to be safer and bearing less risk than those from outside our borders.

to believe their company is safer than others. As a result, time and again we see employees often holding too much stock in the company they work for. One study showed that 8 percent of employees in their sixties have over 90 percent of their retirement savings in their company's stock.[11] We have seen the risks play out in the likes of World-Com or Enron, where many employees saw their life savings evaporate due to overinvestment in their company's stock.*

In general, many investors display an unwarranted sense of security in public companies, whereas the facts paint a different picture. Of the two thousand technology companies that had initial public offerings between 1980 and 2006, less than 5 percent account for 100 percent of the $2 trillion–plus of wealth created through those enterprises.[12] In fact, even a smaller handful within that group is responsible for the lion's share of that total. The other 95 percent of public technology companies serve as painful destroyers of wealth.

The technology sector tends to be more volatile than most, but as Robert Shiller has often pointed out, mutual funds have long been "educating" investors about stocks with their promising prospects and "low risk" to encourage ever-increasing purchases thereof. One notorious example of this is found in James Glassman and Kevin Hassett's book from the turn of the millennium, *Dow 36,000: The New Strategy for Profiting from the Coming Rise in the Stock Market,* which naively argued that there was much money to be made in the early years of the new century, attributing almost fixed-income risk characteristics to public equities.[13] History has ultimately proved Glassman and Hassett dead wrong and, thankfully although surely temporarily, buried the notion that public companies are automatically safer than private companies.

---

* Enron's employees' total 401(k) assets had a shocking 57.73 percent invested in Enron stock as it fell by 98.8 percent in 2001.

Rational Ignorance

Economists have attributed a great deal of poor decision-making to *rational ignorance*. Rational ignorance refers to our conscious and deliberate choice to be ignorant about certain matters because the effort to educate ourselves about those matters appears too difficult or deemed not worth it. In other words, the opportunity cost appears to be too high. And investors may say to themselves, "Why should we understand all the specifics when our investment advisor or broker knows what he is talking about?" We will soon see why this is a dangerous attitude.

Rational ignorance is a term usually used in a political context, referring to voters being ignorant about the people they elect. Voters tend to focus on one or two major issues and ignore the rest. The explanation for this phenomenon is because one person's vote is not enough to sway any election, spending a considerable amount of time to get oneself educated on all the issues makes no economic sense. Any one person's sophistication is not enough to make any material difference to election results. American economist and Nobel Prize winner James M. Buchanan said it best:

> *This greater complexity of political choice is compounded by an inability to gain from any investment in knowledge. In a market setting, a person can gain by storing food during the boom periods; it is a simple task to profit directly from knowledge. In a political setting, however, even if a person has acquired knowledge about the more complex question of "why," there is no way that he can profit from his knowledge because a change in policy will take place only after a majority of people have come to the same conclusion. Consequently, it is rational to be considerably more ignorant about general policy matters than about matters of market choice.*[14]

While Buchanan is right about politics, he is overly generous in his estimation of those who can profit from being less ignorant. Regrettably, in financial services, most people are quite ignorant about the market or have adopted rational ignorance. They may know some things about stock selection, options, some elements of economics, or perhaps even something about real estate. But it's certainly difficult to have both a broad and deep understanding of the investment universe. Therefore, most investors are still clueless about the ways that investment managers and advisors operate, how they get incentivized, and all the ways that investors can find themselves on the short end of the stick.

The fact that politicians try to take advantage of voter ignorance—by making whatever promises need to be made to get elected—is not news. However, we would like to believe that our financial professionals would not do the same, especially since these individuals are often people we personally know, perhaps even members of our community or family, and they know that our investment portfolios are the products of our blood, sweat, and tears and the foundation of our future.

The problem is that marketers and salespeople can take advantage of rational ignorance. It is important to remember that most investments are designed to be sold, not to be owned. Whether these investments are presented as "risk-free" structured products or a security that "can go nowhere but up," investors and advisors should approach even the best-sounding opportunities with a healthy dose of skepticism. This brings to mind the story of a neophyte fisherman who walks into a bait shop, notices all the elaborately decorated lures, and asks the storekeeper if the dressing on all these lures actually attracts more fish. To which the storekeeper quickly responds, "Young man, we don't sell lures to fish."[15] What works and what sells may, in fact, be two different things.

The bottom line here is to get to know what you don't know. Avoiding rational ignorance and baseless discrimination against various asset classes or strategies is imperative for a properly diversified investor.

Changing Roles and Responsibilities

There is another challenge, or set of frustrations, that investors have to overcome. That is accepting and transitioning from having the roles and responsibilities of an entrepreneur, or of any other vocation, to the starkly different roles and responsibilities of investors.*

In this transition, successful entrepreneurs have to move away from having established infrastructure in the form of staff, executive assistance, industry consultants, established suppliers, and many other resources. When they sell the business, they become sole operators trying to make sense of their new roles, and many find their new roles to be disorienting. They don't have the support of their executive assistants and all those employees who have historically fulfilled so many tasks for them.

Entrepreneurs also have to learn new rules of intervention, as they have likely jumped in to fix what is broken when the business went off course. In public markets or long-term investments in general, however, intervention is often uncalled for. Perhaps the most important skill entrepreneurs can learn when it comes to investing is how to sit on their hands when the markets go awry.

Change is not always easy. And in terms of becoming good investors, entrepreneurs must change their perspective of how money is made. They have likely benefited from focusing their attention, concentrating most resources on just one or two strategies and one or two markets, trying to penetrate those as deeply as possible. Investors, on the other hand, aspire to diversify their portfolios and are deliberately trying to get exposure to as many strategies in as many different markets as possible.

---

* The same would be true with anyone that inherited wealth, where one shifts from being a beneficiary to being a steward of wealth.

For entrepreneurs, a single-minded focus and bold moves are often critical for building morale and inspiring the confidence of employees—even if the certainty is not warranted. For investors, however, such narrow focus connotes overconfidence and overconcentration and could be potentially disastrous down the road.

Parenthetically, entrepreneurs are not the only ones who are guilty of this. Various studies suggest that when doctors claimed to be completely certain about a diagnosis, they were wrong 40 percent of the time. In comparable studies, it was demonstrated that when groups of students who claimed there was only a 1 percent chance of them being wrong, they would be wrong 27 percent of the time.[16] Similarly, if you had asked the traders at Lehman in 2007 how likely they would rate the possibility of their demise twelve months down the road, it is doubtful that even 1 percent of them would have acknowledged it as a possibility.* Even everyday people fall prey to this sense of extreme optimism and overconfidence. Research suggests that 64 percent of Americans believe they are going to heaven, while only 0.5 percent believe they will end up in hell.[17]

For individuals who have amassed great wealth or for successful entrepreneurs, overconfidence manifests itself as overreliance on the domain that produced their wealth and relying on that same sector, industry, or asset type to preserve their wealth. However, this can be a colossal risk to one's nest egg. Any sector can have a down year or a down decade, and it may just be the year or decade you most need your capital. Getting exposed to many asset classes, learning new things, and stepping out of one's comfort zone will limit one's ability to be overconfident and overconcentrated.

---

* Incidentally, leverage is a steroid to overconfidence and often results in a deadly combination. Lehman Brothers was among its most notorious addicts. Just prior to the financial crisis, Lehman Brothers' financial statements showed accounting leverage of 30.7 times the stockholders' equity, and bankruptcy examiner Anton Valukas later determined that the true accounting leverage was significantly higher, having been understated due to dubious accounting.

So what do experts advise to avoid overconfidence? Consult a woman. Terrance Odean and Brad Barber studied investing practices according to gender. They discovered that women are superior long-term investors because they made changes to their portfolios 67 percent less frequently than men did and were far better at avoiding overconfidence.[18] As a result, women have outperformed men by an average of 1.4 percent per year.[19]

To be an investor, it is important to step outside your comfort zone, to continually educate yourself, and to engage in professional development to better do your job. To do so, there are some basic starting points. For starters, read the books, articles, and case studies of successful investors (e.g., Berkshire Hathaway reports). Subsequently, develop familiarity with all the strategies, concepts, and investment terms that scare you. Once you have achieved some sense of fluency in the strategies, read through a few offering memorandums, *including all the fine print*. It will give you a good sense of what the marketing material will not. Throughout, ask questions relentlessly. When it comes to your wealth, there is no such thing as a dumb question. Blind trust is the enemy of investors. Lastly, start cultivating an investment philosophy. It will pay unexpected dividends as you go along.

With all of that said, no investor should venture forth alone. The velocity of change and innovation in financial services will make it difficult for any one person to keep up with every new financial strategy or product offering. This is sort of like building a car while driving it at the same time. Taking a seasoned, trusted advisor along for the ride will ensure you don't break down along the way.

A foolish faith in authority is the worst enemy of truth.

—Albert Einstein

Independence

It's important to remember that the rest of the world does not share your unique goals, needs, and aspirations. Accordingly, the decisions and concerns of the masses should be of limited relevance to you. You must remember this simple fact to avoid being swept up by the noise of the market and its captivating banter. This means ignoring what you see on Bloomberg, ignoring stock tips from golf club buddies or cocktail party friends, and avoiding checking stock prices every five minutes. Instead, you should focus on a disciplined investment process and stick to the plan you have developed for your specific needs through both calm and turbulent times. This, however, is no easy task. It is even harder if you are a professional money manager or broker whose job security hinges on performance not being poorer than the market in any year, quarter, or month. These money managers are often forced to trade off between maximizing the performance of their clients' portfolios over the long term and maximizing the value of the money management business today. Unfortunately, the two can stand in stark contrast to one another, and any short-term aspiration (i.e., don't risk losing the assets under management) will likely lead to index imitation (i.e., play it safe and follow the herd). As John Maynard Keynes famously said, "Worldly wisdom teaches that it is better for one's reputation to fail conventionally than to succeed unconventionally." Much like we've seen in the natural world,* this

---

* Researchers Carl Anderson and John Bartholdi illustrate the consequences of this behavior in the natural world through the marches of army ants: "A group of worker ants, which are essentially blind, sometimes separates from the colony. Since no individual ant has any idea how to relocate the rest of the colony, all the ants rely on a simple decisions rule: follow the ant in front of you. If enough individuals follow the strategy (i.e., they reach the tipping point), they develop a circular mill, where ants follow each other around in circles until death." Anderson, C., & Bartholdi, III, J. J. (2000). Centralized versus decentralized control in manufacturing: lessons from social insects.

blind tailing of the pack has repeatedly led investors on a path toward capital attrition.

Obviously, investors and advisors have the capacity to think independently. They simply fall into the trap of groupthink or herd mentality and adopt other people's mistakes. Taking an independent view is difficult for two reasons. First of all, if you are wrong when everyone else is wrong, it is not the end of the world. Your bonus may be in jeopardy, but not your job. On the other hand, if you're wrong when everybody else is right, you can kiss your colleagues good-bye. Second, being independently minded is difficult because it actually hurts.

Research has shown that only the best investors have managed to ignore the madness of the masses, and, every so often, even they may succumb as well. The challenge isn't merely intellectual defiance to withstand the sentiments of the masses. According to the research of Gregory Berns, a neuroeconomist at Emory University, it may actually be painful. Based on his findings, it appears that when a person stands up against the face of popular opinion, there is a flare-up in the amygdala. This flare-up occurs in the exact part of the brain that recognizes physical pain.[20] Effectively, being contrarian may actually be sending painful messages to the brain. This may explain why there are so few successful, truly contrarian investors.

One of the ways of avoiding the noise and the pain of being independently minded is to simply remove oneself from the fray. There's a reason why the world's greatest living investor is in Omaha and North America's best-performing pension plan is in North Dakota.[21] And it's not just your investments that will flourish but your entire demeanor. According to Harvard University professor Shawn Achor, removing the noise is one of the most critical elements in ensuring inner peace and personal fulfillment.[22] So over the long term, independence may very well prove to be priceless.

Understanding History

As Yogi Berra once said, "It's déjà vu all over again." Recurrent episodes of speculative booms and busts have always been a part of history. One of the starkest examples of past lessons comes from the tulip mania of the seventeenth century. The average price of a single bulb allegedly grew to exceed the annual income of a skilled worker. Imagine today a tulip bulb selling for over $40,000! Clearly, the price was neither sustainable nor reflective of the true economics of tulips.* It was a bubble of epic proportions. After a few months, the price normalized (i.e., dropped all the way down to the price of a potato peel), and the individuals who had traded in their entire estates for tulip bulbs lost everything.

Most bubbles and busts are not as dramatic. Some simply take on the air of a fad and compel investors to ignore true value in the process. In the late 1960s and early 1970s, for example, there was quite a bit of exuberance around the so-called nifty fifty. These were essentially deemed "no-lose" or "one-decision" stocks, which one could buy and hold forever. Initially, the prices of these stocks skyrocketed—some as high as ninety times earnings. Less than a year after the stock market crashed in 1973, however, investors lost their enthusiasm, and virtually all these companies hit profound lows. Even more interesting is that in the thirty years that followed, this group as a whole (with Walmart as a notable exception) did substantially worse than the S&P 500 or any other popular index.[23]

The lesson of most sizzling growth stories seems that at some point they tend to come back down to earth. Yet somehow investors cannot get their heads around that. Michael Mauboussin points out that

---

* This example of herd mentality is unfortunately quite common in investing. Contrary to the most basic economic principles where price increases reduce demand, in public markets, price increases in a particular stock only increase the demand of that stock. Eventually, however, the true economics of price-demand surface, the bubble pops, and costly investment lessons are learned.

the S&P Index generated a return of 8.2 percent in the twenty years ended 2009. The average mutual fund saw a return of about 7 percent, reflecting the performance drag of fees. But the average investor earned a return of less than 6 percent, about two-thirds of the market's return and less than the very funds they invested in. This phenomenon has been called the dumb money effect. On average, investors actually do worse than the very funds they're in because they are chasing yesterday's story. They put money after markets (or funds) that have been doing well and pull money out after markets (or funds) that have been doing poorly. This is the opposite of the behavior you would expect from investors who understand historic trends of booms, busts and reversions to the mean.[24]

According to Professors Amit Goyal and Sunil Wahal, institutional investors, such as pension plans and foundations, did not fare much better. In a study on how 3,400 institutions made their decisions to hire and fire investment managers over a ten-year period,[25] they discovered that institutions hired investment managers after they had generated superior returns with post-hiring excess returns reverting back to zero. And while investment managers were fired for many different reasons, poor performance proved to be the number-one cause on the list. Invariably, after being fired, these very managers proceeded to once again achieve meaningful excess returns.[26]

We are again reminded that drawdowns, as bad as they may be, do not necessarily warrant running for the hills. In fact, they may present unique opportunities. On that infamous Black Monday crash, which produced the worst one-day drawdown in market history, great fortunes were made. For institutional investors that maintained a proper perspective, the precipitous drop in 1987 that forced them to rebalance their bond-equity mix was a gift. It forced them to buy a great deal of stocks at obscenely cheap prices, and once prices rebounded, they were the largest beneficiaries. The same is often true of money managers who have had one or two difficult years but otherwise strong prospects and fundamentals.

History is replete with similar stories, whether it's tulips in Holland, the South Sea Company in Britain, or the tech bubble in the United States. For those who get acquainted with economic history and understand its lessons, dramatic booms and busts become hardly surprising.

In *The Signal and the Noise*, Nate Silver points out that, as early as 2000, Robert Shiller referenced the housing bubble in his book *Irrational Exuberance*. Other economists started writing about it in 2002, and in June of 2005, *The Economist* labeled it the "biggest bubble in history."[27] The bubble was being written about in every newspaper or periodical, and Google searches for "housing bubble" increased tenfold from January 2004 to the summer of 2005.[28] The financial crisis of 2008, with the bursting of the housing bubble at its core, was something that common sense and an understanding of financial history could have averted. Regrettably, the masses have neither, so the chips fell where they did. There were some, however, that did have common sense and employed the lessons of history.* They had the discipline to protect themselves against losses; some even made money in the process.

Investment Philosophy

Of course, history is not the entire story. As Warren Buffett points out, "If past history is all there was to the game, the richest people would be librarians." Besides a good understanding of financial history, virtually all extraordinary investors have a well-thought-out investment philosophy that coherently incorporates all the elements

---

* Incidentally, the 2008 financial crisis presented us with the gift of manager selection. It allowed us to see who actually had common sense and who went with the crowd. The crisis also helped us to better evaluate which funds would perform under adverse conditions. Granted, every financial crisis is different, and every strategy will behave differently under distinct market conditions, but it is useful to see how both managers and funds faired in 2008.

we have outlined thus far. It need not be original or bulletproof, but it should be consistent, withstanding the vagaries of market sentiment and proving to be right more often than it is wrong.

Failure to develop an investment philosophy can have catastrophic consequences for even the most brilliant individuals. One notable and dramatic example is Sir Isaac Newton. Newton, one of the most significant scientists in history, is best known for defining many of the foundational principals of the physical universe, particularly in regard to the laws of motion and gravitation. He is less known for his involvement in the science of currency (i.e., its alchemy), his curiosity about the history of money, and his keen interest in the economics of the monetary system.[29] This interest undoubtedly led to his appointment to the distinguished post of warden and master of Britain's Royal Mint. However, despite his extraordinary intelligence and his interest in financial markets, he failed to formulate a sensible investment philosophy. That is why in the summer of 1720, during the delirious exuberance of the South Sea Bubble and even after proclaiming, "I can calculate the movement of stars, but not the madness of men," he proceeded to invest £20,000, the bulk of his life's savings, in the stock of the South Sea Company near the peak of the market.[30]

Developing an investment philosophy may be one of the most useful exercises an investor can embark on. It may take years to develop and refine, but it will prove invaluable when markets or valuations cease to make sense and public fervor takes over.

Take Your Time

In 1764, Thomas Bayes bequeathed one of the greatest gifts to investors. The essence of his contribution is outlined in Bayes's work *An Essay Towards Solving a Problem in the Doctrine of Chance*. Putting the technical math aside, his basic message is that, given the infinite factors contributing to movements in financial markets, the best we can do is a probability distribution. One cannot say with certainty that markets will rise 8 percent. One could, however, potentially determine that, based on historic trends, there is a 20 percent chance of markets rising 8–12 percent, a 40 percent chance of markets rising 1–7 percent, and a 30 percent chance of markets falling 1–7 percent, and finally a 10 percent chance of losses or gains exceeding those numbers.

This approach, however, is in sharp contrast with the majority of forecasters, speculators, and market timers attempting to convince you of their confidence in the markets. Savvy investors and advisors don't rely on forecasts or predictions of the future. Instead, they take their time analyzing all potential risks and the probability of those risks materializing, and they carefully identify ways to mitigate those exposures.

Behavioral psychologists have demonstrated that there are other benefits for taking one's time to consider probabilities—namely, it will help one avoid being subjected to harmful biases and poor choices. Researchers Eric Gold and Gordon Hester at Carnegie Mellon University exposed our irrationality in spotting trends.[31] They showed that if someone flipped a coin and it fell on heads four consecutive times, the person will assume the probability of the fifth toss being tails is now higher.* This is, of course, despite the fact that the probability of the fifth, sixth, seventh, and every toss thereafter still has a 50 percent chance of landing on heads.

Humans are by nature pattern seekers even where no pattern exists. In a fascinating study, subjects were asked to guess whether a light would flash at the top or the bottom of a computer screen. Unbeknownst to the participants, researchers set 80 percent of all flashes to randomly appear at the top. The study was done on adults, young children, and even animals (pigeons and mice). Once animals

---

* This phenomenon has been referred to as the *gambler's fallacy*, which will be referenced again later in the book.

or young children realized that flashes were predominantly at the top, they proceeded to choose the top of the screen for all successive guesses, effectively getting the answer correct 80 percent of the time. Adults and older children, however, were not content with just guessing the top each time and tried to figure out the pattern in which the light flashed. As a result, they only guessed correctly 64 percent of the time.[32] Thus, our search for patterns often prompts us to neglect or discount probabilities.

There is a solution to our relentless pattern seeking. In the coin toss example, the experimenters discovered that if the subject stepped away after the fourth coin toss and returned some time later, the subject's perception of probabilities reverted back to fifty-fifty.[33] This suggests that one simple way to protect yourself from being subject to unhealthy biases, looking for patterns where none exist, or generally poor investment decisions is simply to take your time.

Social Autonomy

Social autonomy is perhaps most difficult for investors to achieve. We all have individuals in our lives to whom we owe favors. We all have family and friends that guilt us, often against our better judgment, into getting involved in this, that, or the other. While that may be fine in many endeavors (e.g., charities, local baseball leagues, or cohosting a party) and be seen as simply the cost of friendship, in investing, these social forces are usually inconsistent with best-practice wealth preservation.

One of challenges I face after a new client has retained our services and asked us to analyze their existing portfolio is honestly evaluating the socially motivated investment. Such an investment could have come from a nephew, a neighbor, a childhood friend, a golfing buddy, a church member, or anyone else who lives in that individual's social universe. These investments can sometimes be extremely attractive opportunities, as they come with the benefit of dealing with individuals you know and trust. Unfortunately, people may also invest with those in their social universe *only because* they are part of their social universe. In other words, the investment is not looked at objectively and may be considered completely unacceptable if it had been brought by anyone else.

The absence of such social autonomy will invariably compromise returns. There's a sea of data on the topic. In one famous study on 3,510 venture capitalists entitled *The Cost of Friendship*, researchers at Harvard University demonstrated that affinity-based partnerships (i.e., investing with friends) dramatically reduced the probability of investment success. Conversely, ability-based partnerships (i.e., finding time-tested and best-fitting investments or investment managers) greatly increased the probability of investment success.[34]

The way we address this challenge with new clients is by employing some of the strategies we will outline in the section on benchmarks. For now, suffice it to say that we compare the performance and terms of their socially motivated investments to the broader universe of players employing a similar strategy. Quite often, there's a sizeable gap between the two (usually translating into millions of dollars in opportunity costs). I then ask the new client, *Are you prepared to continue forgoing this amount for the sake of this relationship?* If the investment is with a close friend of the client, and I happen to be in a contentious mood that day, I may also ask, *Do you think your friendship is dependent on this? And if so, then how real of a friendship is it?*

This phenomenon is as true with specific investments as it is with investment advisors. Whether we like it or not, capital preservation requires us to make difficult choices, often forgoing that which is easy, accessible, and socially convenient. If you are not prepared to make those difficult choices, then there isn't much use in continuing to read this book, as best-practice investing requires a rational, rather than an emotional, approach. If, however, you are prepared to make the difficult decisions to ensure your long-term investment success, we can turn to the next section on the hows of identifying the right partners in preservation.

KEY TAKEAWAYS FROM PART II

- Most investors have inflated views of their investment abilities and prospects for success. Humility, however, is necessary for a healthy investment dynamic.
- We attribute safety to that which is familiar and attribute riskiness to that which is not.
- Diversification, however, is also important for a healthy investment dynamic. Overconcentration is a destroyer of wealth.
- Education is the key to opening up opportunities that are foreign to us.
- Avoid the noise from social and professional sources. Become familiar enough with financial history to think independently when markets get rocky.
- An educated investment philosophy can serve as a ballast in tumultuous times.

PART III

THE ADVISOR

> *The greatest obstacle to discovery is not ignorance—*
> *it is the illusion of knowledge.*
>
> —Daniel J. Boorstin

Getting Help

Financial education may sound simple, and you may take it as a given that financial literacy is helpful in supporting better investment decisions. And it is. But the story is a bit more nuanced. Research seems to indicate that financial education has negligible—if any—impact on investors. In a survey of 168 papers, covering 201 studies, even large educational interventions proved to have limited effect over time.[1] What has proven to be effective, however, is when investment education is provided just in time, at the very moment where one is in the position to make investment decisions.

Regrettably, there is no *Consumer Reports* of investments and no easy shortcuts. To invest successfully, investors needs to find the resources that will help them make better investment decisions. This is difficult, as investors fall in love with investment ideas or become enamored by charismatic individuals. These positive emotions lead to negative outcomes. Donald G. MacGregor has shown that when an investment opportunity has a strong affective impact on us, we tend to overweigh the outcome rather than the probabilities of success.[2] For example, when one imagines the prospect of winning the lottery, there is strong associative sentiments with the idea of newfound wealth and how a new, wealthy life might look. As a result, how many lottery tickets are bought will hardly be impacted by whether the chances of winning are one in five million or one in fifty million (even though winning the latter is ten times less likely). Similarly, when investors feel good about an investment, they tend to perceive the risks as being lower and the prospect of returns as being higher despite probabilities to the contrary.[3]

There may, however, be times when our guts, instincts, or emotions have something to add to our investing. Researchers have demonstrated our subconscious can often pick up on trends—positive or negative—even before our psyche does. In a well-known study, Antonio Damasio, a neuroscientist at the University of Southern California and an expert in somatic indicators, put several decks of cards in front of test subjects. One was a winning deck, one was a losing deck, and one was purely random. The subject had to pick cards until he or she could confidently say which one was which. In almost every experiment, long before the subject was able to consciously articulate which deck was a winner or loser, the body had already recognized the losing deck, and the subject would exhibit symptoms of stress or anxiety whenever he or she reached for the losing deck.[4] Taking together the research of Mac-Gregor and Damasio, it would seem that while a decision *to* invest should not be done purely using our instincts, there may be times when our gut can help inform us where *not to* invest.

Notwithstanding this occasional intuition, few should venture down the path of investing alone. Even those who have broad and deep investment experience or knowledge should still find some completely objective partner in preservation with proven experience and a robust understanding of the investment world who can at the very least serve as a sounding board. There is a reason the world's greatest athletes and performers all have coaches and trainers, irrespective of how veteran they may be.[5] As Picasso once said, "One should not be one's own connoisseur."

The Four Roles of an Advisor

There are four core roles that an advisor may play:

1. Planning
2. Sourcing and selecting
3. Researching
4. Managing

Each of these roles has distinct responsibilities, and investors must ensure that they have each of these bases effectively covered.

PLANNING

Vince Lombardi, the legendary coach of the Green Bay Packers, has often said that there is no such thing as a perfect game. You cannot control the weather, the referees, the injuries, or any number of other variables. You can, however, have a perfect practice with a plan to respond to any eventuality. The same applies to investing. There is no way to anticipate any number of factors that can affect an investment, but if a portfolio is properly planned and prepared, the impact of the unexpected will be minimized.

In the first chapter of *In Search of the Prime Quadrant*, we outlined all the reasons why a robust plan in the form of an investment policy statement (IPS) is indispensable. Here I will provide much more depth as to what constitutes an IPS and how to create one.

Let us first refresh ourselves on why a fully developed IPS is absolutely vital before proceeding with any investment discussions or decisions. Take a look at the four images below and see if you can guess what all these edifices have in common.

If you guessed that these were all built by, arguably, the greatest living architect, Frank Owen Gehry, you would be half-right. All four of these buildings were designed by Frank Gehry, but all four of these buildings are also examples of poor planning. The Ray and Maria Stata Center at MIT (top left) did not consider winter conditions and the cascading design creates rows of sharp icicles that fall like daggers on passersby below.* The Peter B. Lewis Building at Case Western Reserve University (top right) did not consider weather at all. It has been likened to a tanning mirror, emitting extreme heat during the summer, and melting snow on the sloping roof into streams of slush that slid onto the heads of unsuspecting pedestrians below, effectively rendering the surrounding area un-walkable. The northwest corner of the Walt Disney Concert Hall (bottom right), was designed with such highly polished mirrorlike panels that the reflective surface created an uncomfortable glare and heat for the condominiums across the street.

---

* MIT sued Gehry and received $1.5 million to offset some of the costs of fixing the problems.

According to a third-party assessment, the reflection created hot spots on the sidewalks of as much as 140°F (60°C).* Finally, shortly after its opening, the Guggenheim Museum in Bilbao (bottom left) had to deal with unattractive brown stains on the titanium exterior of the museum. It turned out that these stains were naturally occurring and would come to cost the museum tens of thousands of dollars in annual cleaning.†

With added forethought, every one of these challenges could have been mitigated or entirely eliminated. That is precisely why planning is the most important part of the construction process, and a lack of planning may tarnish even the most impressive of talents or achievements. Sound investing requires an understanding of the fundamentals as well as well-crafted architecture. In fact, according to one survey of international high-net-worth investors, some 57 percent said that their single biggest regret was not having set up a comprehensive financial plan earlier in life.[6]

The point here is that even the greatest designers, artisans, architects, and technicians will falter with a poorly crafted plan. The same is true in investing. Even with the greatest investments, it is possible to have very poor results without the proper plan.

Creating the Investment Policy Statement

I often tell my clients that they should think about their investment planning as they would think about building the home of their dreams. In this part, I am going to give you a quick and rather simplified overview on how to go about it. Pay close attention, as this step, the creation of the IPS, is, in my view, the most important component of the investment process.

---

* In addition, it increased the risk of traffic accidents due to blinding sunlight to oncoming cars.
† The horribly embarrassed museum officials scrambled to figure out how to remedy the situation, but the gigantic, curved, and difficult-to-reach panels made cleaning the stains an ongoing (and costly) headache.

While an IPS is employed by the world's most accomplished and disciplined investors,* it is no less beneficial or crucial for private investors. In fact, good planning and exceptional strategy can turn the ordinary into the spectacular. Whether in battle, in sports, in business, or investing, one does not need to be the brightest, the fastest, or the best financially endowed. One can do well with few other resources but an excellent plan.

How Do You Do It?

Constructing an IPS is not much different from constructing a home. No one in his or her right mind would simply show a picture of an attractive house to an architect and proceed on that basis alone. Instead, he or she would diligently discuss and consider every minute aspect of the home, the possible uses of each room, the required amenities, the plumbing, the electrical system, and countless other details. Creating the blueprint for one's investing (i.e., the IPS) is no different. Before you start to feel overwhelmed, let me calm your nerves by pointing out that at the most basic level there are only four steps in the creation of an IPS.

1. Figure out your personal needs and aspirations.
2. Determine your personal constraints.
3. Outline your operational plan.
4. Develop your monitoring plan.

Each of these steps cascades from one to the other and back. Skipping over one will have detrimental effects on your long-term goals. Make sure no step is omitted and that the execution is holistically synchronized.

---

* These are some of the largest pension plans, endowments, and insurance companies who start with an end in mind and who have consistently met their investment goals over an investment horizon, providing stability and results for their beneficiaries.

Step One: Figure Out Your Needs and Aspirations

In order to zero in on needs and aspirations, it helps to think of them in terms of five months, five years, and five decades. What you want to accomplish at each point will be different, and each stage needs to be carefully considered.

To do this involves getting a handle on all current and projected fixed expenditures, as well as all current and projected variable expenditures. These may include a child's wedding, buying a summer home, or a major philanthropic commitment.* Not all of these are predictable, but to the extent one can chart them out, one's plan will be better tailored for them.

First, these needs and aspirations must be quantifiable and precise. For example, "I want to provide for my family's full income of $350,000 per year on an after-tax basis and preserve at least $20 million inflation protected for my grandchildren."

Second, you need to actually do the math to figure out exactly what return you will need to get there. Then you need to write this number down and commit to not venture out any further on the risk spectrum beyond what it will take to achieve this number. This may seem exceptionally simple, but very few individuals actually take the time to make this determination.

Finally, every investment decision should be made on the basis of what role it will play in your portfolio. There are many people chasing after talented investment managers or interesting deals. However, being successful at finding one of these talented managers or interesting deals should not overshadow the IPS. No matter how rare or elusive, should these opportunities not be consistent with the mandate of the IPS, participating in them will decrease the likelihood of one's

---

* It is important that the objectives being spelled out are thorough and multifaceted. They should involve and include even those needs or aspirations that are outside the realm of the traditional scope of finances (e.g., philanthropy or community involvement).

long-term success. Ask yourself, "In the bigger scheme of things, how will it bring me closer to my needs or aspirations?" If you can't answer that with meaningful confidence, forgo the investment.

Step Two: Determine Your Personal Constraints

Needs and aspirations help define constraints. For example, if someone could definitively tell you that you will live fifty more years, you would approach life differently from how you would if you knew you had five more years to live. Similarly, the parameters of every investment we make must be in complete harmony with our needs and aspirations. These parameters include such things as tolerance for volatility, cash-flow requirements from the capital (i.e., paying regular expenses), and special liquidity needs (i.e., the summer home of your dreams). They will also involve such factors as the investment time horizon, taxes,* or shifts in one's financial circumstances (e.g., retiring or selling a business).

Savings rates should also be considered. Savings may sound like it does not belong to the realm of investing, but studies have shown that higher-income earners and high-net-worth individuals are actually weaker savers than those with less than $140,000 of annual income.[7] On a relative basis, many affluent individuals and high-income earners are actually less prepared for retirement than their middle-class counterparts.

North Americans as a whole are inferior savers to most developing countries. According to the Organization for Economic Co-operation and Development, our savings rates are now around 3 percent. By comparison, in China, the savings rate is 38 percent, and India's population saves just under 35 percent of its income. Investors

---

* Taxes may be your biggest investment expense, so just as you must know the difference between gross and net returns on investments, you must know the difference between your gross and net after-tax returns. The tax tail should not generally wag the investment dog, but one should be well informed of the tax considerations (i.e., the cost base, capital gains, and opportunities for tax exemption or deferral).

with any form of income should be mindful of what needs to be put aside for retirement or a rainy day.

Taxes

Over 220 years ago, Ben Franklin warned us that "nothing can be said to be certain, except death and taxes." But even today most investors fail to recognize how much of their returns are eaten up by tax inefficiencies. Mutual funds, for example, have historically erased between 1.5 percent and 2.5 percent of return per annum due to their frequent turnover in assets.[8] To put that in perspective, these inefficiencies can erase almost 25 percent of one's total return on investment. In even more extreme scenarios, tax inefficiency resulting from assets being held in the wrong structures have almost entirely wiped out the returns. For example, on several occasions, new clients came to us with a preexisting portfolio of wonderful, US-based real estate investments. The problem was that they were done through a limited liability company (LLC). They simply didn't know that LLCs can be toxic for Canadian taxpayers, as the Canada Revenue Agency views them as corporations rather than pass-through entities. This creates double taxation issues, forcing investors to pay as much as 65 percent to 70 percent in taxes on their investments. That's the price of forgetting that the after-tax returns are all that matter.

Besides being more efficient, investors often fail to adopt simple, proactive strategies that can significantly reduce the tax bill. Common examples would include tax-loss harvesting, ensuring that assets providing income (such as REITs) are in tax-deferred accounts, using appreciated assets (especially those with really low cost-basis) to fulfill charitable commitments, or converting nondeductible debt into deductible debt.*

---

* As interest payments on money that's borrowed for investment purposes is tax deductible whereas interest on other debt (i.e., home mortgage) is generally not tax deductible.

Naturally, tax decisions should not interfere with a fundamental analysis of an investment's merits, but those who are mindful of their tax constraints and take advantage of tax-mitigating strategies are able to significantly improve returns. The reality is few investors have the interest, patience, or expertise in navigating the tax code. That is why it is imperative for advisors to have at least a basic fluency in the tax implications of common investment vehicles, structures, and strategies.

Step Three: Operational Plan

The operational plan is really where the rubber meets the road. It has three primary components: cash allocation, roles and responsibilities, and asset allocation.

Cash Allocation

Cash allocation refers to how much cash we need to keep our options open and take advantage of unique opportunities and how much cash we need to maintain personal stability and safety. We generally advise our clients to have at least two years' worth of living expenses in cash with the possibility of having a portion of the cash reserve (up to one year's worth) allocated to safe, short-term opportunities. It may be frustrating to have unproductive cash sitting on the sidelines, but as Warren Buffett, who is known for holding extraordinary cash reserves, once said, "Our capital is underutilized. It's a painful condition to be in—but not as painful as doing something stupid."

Operationally, cash should be managed in a way that is holistic and strategic, avoiding the fairly common *mental accounting bias*. This bias manifests when people treat different pools of cash differently for no logical reason. For example, individuals might have one account for spending and another account for savings, one account in the United States and one in Canada, or one personal account and one corporate account. As a result, they may not think of their assets holistically, leading to poor asset allocation. Often people sit on more cash than they thought, and sometimes the opposite is also true. Cash, like every other asset, needs to consolidate on a centralized balance sheet where one can responsibly manage the entirety of one's capital and make every decision in a proper context.

Roles and Responsibilities

It is important to spell out exactly who does what. If there are different family members involved in the investment process, then the roles and responsibilities of those family members should be articulated. If there is an independent foundation, board, or trustee, everyone should be clear as to their roles in investment decisions.

The operational plan should also outline in fairly detailed fashion how you interact with your investment consultant and your various investment managers or brokers. What do each of them provide you with? How do they report to you? What do they expect from you?

Asset Allocation

Since the premiere of the movie *Moneyball*, there have been many that have tried to adopt the strategies* of former Oakland Athletics' general manager, Billy Beane. Many have almost stopped worrying about getting the best picks. Instead, they use better strategies and innovative game plans to meet their goals. Alongside Billy Beane, Michael Lewis has written about another, much less prominent, pioneer of this approach, the Texas Tech football coach Mike Leach. Despite playing highly competitive teams, Leach managed to win over 70 percent of his games with few players who were considered first-rate material by

---

* Michael "Billy" Beane popularized the field of sabermetrics, which involves statistically analyzing players on the basis of how they contributed to wins rather than using more traditional measures, such as batting averages and runs batted in (RBIs).

the scIouts.[9] He did this by frequently changing the formations, shifting the matchups, and forcing opponents to constantly shift defensive strategies until he exposed the other team's weaknesses.[10] There are similar experiences to be found in basketball, where researcher Wayne Winston proved that teams can win tournaments simply by controlling the order of when they play which teams.[11]

Although they are vastly different fields, the ideas behind sabermetrics are the very same ideas behind a robust asset allocation. Study after study has shown that over 90 percent of the performance of a portfolio can be explained by asset allocation.[12] In fact, a study by Eugene F. Fama Jr. looking at thirty-one institutional pension funds over a range of six to twelve years suggests that as much as 97 percent of performance is attributed to asset class structure.[13]

Simply put, asset allocation refers to how much of each type of investment we should have in a portfolio. It often requires trade-offs between volatility, liquidity, and returns. Part of the process of allocating involves simulating the possible outcomes of different asset allocations, often referred to as the Monte Carlo simulation, based on historical data. This is a stress test to see what happens to our plans in the event of any number of factors, such as high inflation or low equity returns. The asset allocation is run through over ten thousand possible scenarios and, based on those results, provides the probability of achieving financial goals under the stated constraints. This means that the asset allocation can be adjusted until a comfort level is achieved for the best-case scenario, the worst-case scenario, and the likelihood of meeting the goals.

Diversification

Most investors cannot possibly achieve their goals without exposure to a diversity of asset classes.[14] For investors who would like to see their portfolios stand up in almost all market conditions, there is nothing more fundamental than allocating funds across different and varied asset classes where value is derived from fundamentally different sources.

There is no shortage of data that shows why this is important. The most common reason is that there may be decades of certain asset classes producing negative to flat returns. Take, for example, the Canadian real estate market in the early 1990s or North American equities in the first decade of this millennium or even most of the years between 1960 and 1980. There are countless other examples, and those unfamiliar with the topic should begin by reading chapter 5 of *In Search of the Prime Quadrant.*

For the purposes of wealth preservation, the goal should be exposure across a wide array of asset classes. And to get exposure to these asset classes, one must first understand option sets and be able to distinguish between them. The table provides some examples of major asset classes and sub-asset classes an investor may be exposed to. These are the potential building blocks of an investment plan.

ASSET CLASSES	EXAMPLES OF SUB-ASSET CLASSES
Cash and Cash Alternatives	Domestic currency; foreign currency; money markets*; short-duration government bonds; cashable GICs
Public Equities	Long-only; long-biased; short-biased; event-driven; sector; geography; growth; value
Private Equity	Leveraged buyout; growth capital; venture capital; secondary funds; direct co-investment
Fixed Income	Investment-grade sovereign bonds; investment-grade corporate bonds

---

* While highly liquid money market funds, T-bills, and cashable GICs would technically be categorized as Credit, they can also serve as fairly conservative cash alternatives. The technicality is important, however, because there have been cases of GIC defaults.

Credit	High-yield (i.e., non-investment grade); mortgages; distressed debt; bank loans; mezzanine lending
Real Assets	Commercial, industrial, and residential real estate; farmland; timberland; infrastructure; commodities; and precious metals
Uncorrelated	Long/short; global macro; commodity trading advisors; arbitrage; relative value; multi-strategy

Truly anything can happen at any time, and while we cannot predict the unexpected, we can certainly immunize ourselves (to an extent) from its impact. Thus, only by diversifying across most of the asset classes can an investor achieve the highest probability of preserving capital through all market conditions.

Some of the best investors in the world consistently plan for the unexpected. Howard Marks, the legendary investor and chairman of Oaktree Capital Management, once shared a story that deeply impacted his investment philosophy. He talked about a particular gambler who once heard about a race with only one horse in it. He saw it as a no-lose proposition, so he ran straight to the bookie and bet everything he had on the horse. Halfway around the track, the horse jumped over the fence and ran away, taking with it the gambler's last penny.[15]

Research has shown that price changes do not follow a normal distribution. Extreme events happen considerably more frequently than their standard deviation* model might suggest. Michael

---

* Standard deviation is the measure of dispersion from the average annual return. In other words, it is the statistical measurement of historical volatility. An investment that is highly volatile will have a high standard deviation and is expected to deviate more drastically from its average return. Conversely, an investment that is less volatile will have a lower standard deviation and is expected to deviate much less from its average annual return.

Mauboussin uses the example of Black Monday in October 1987, the result of which was twenty standard deviations away from the mean.[16] Roger Lowenstein, the author of *When Genius Failed: The Rise and Fall of Long-Term Capital Management*, quotes Jens Carsten Jackwerth and Mark Rubinstein, saying:

> *Economists later figured that, on the basis of the market's historical volatility, had the market been open every day since the creation of the Universe, the odds would still have been against its falling that much in a single day. In fact, had the life of the Universe been repeated one billion times, such a crash would still have been theoretically "unlikely."*

Other legendary investors have molded their investment philosophy around the unexpected. For Nassim Taleb, author of *The Black Swan*, every investment decision is painted by the prospect of the unexpected. He shares a story of a turkey that has been fed by a farmer for one thousand consecutive days. By this point in time, he has come to accept the fact that when the farmer shows up, he (the turkey) will get fed. To the turkey's awful surprise, on day 1,001, just before Thanksgiving, the farmer arrives not with feed but an ax.

Taleb is echoing the words of David Hume[17] and Bertrand Russell,* who claimed that inductive reasoning is a poor predictor of the future.[18] Time and time again, we are humbled by the unpredictability of the market. Things that we couldn't imagine yesterday can easily become today's reality.

Daniel Kahneman, psychologist and author, demonstrates that people will envision risk to be only as bad as something they've witnessed or experienced. They cannot grasp the concept of something worse occurring until it does and thereby rarely prepare accordingly.[19]

---

* In his example, Russell referred to a chicken—not a turkey.

In 2008, the "safe assets" surprising us were in real estate, including all the financial vehicles that supported the supposedly stable housing market. More than half of the losses of the global financial crisis in 2008 were attributed to collateralized debt obligations (CDOs) of the housing market. Of these CDOs, over 28 percent of those rated AAA by at least one of the top three US rating agencies had defaulted.[20] These investments were considered safe by all accounts, and housing prices were projected to go nowhere but up. There was no convincing the average American that over the long term returns on single-family housing were not greater than the after-tax rate of inflation.[21] In fact, Nobel Prize–winning economist Robert Shiller found that over the 114-year period culminating in 2004, the real prices of homes were mostly flat or declining, providing a total increase of 66 percent, or an annual increase of 0.4 percent, which is far below the rate of inflation.[22]

Today, the "safe assets" surprising us are bonds. While 2000 through 2010 has been referred to as the "lost decade" for stocks, it has certainly been the "discovered decade" for bonds. From the year 2000 to 2010, bonds have been the best-performing asset class at just under 7 percent per annum. Today, we take for granted how much of a bond bull market the last thirty years have been. If one looks at bonds in a proper historic context, one will see that in 1916, in the midst of World War I, the Russian army was borrowing money at 6.36 percent. In 1922, amid extreme hyperinflation, Berlin was borrowing at just over 6 percent. Even the army of the Confederate States was borrowing at 6.7 percent in 1861. It can be said, then, that the bond market in times of relative calm, notwithstanding the crash of 2008, has been as good as it gets. Once an asset approaches "as good as it gets," however, there is usually only one place left to go. As interest rates rise and the Federal Reserve cuts back their quantitative easing programs, the illusion of "safe assets" will eventually fade, leaving shocked and disappointed investors in its wake. This was foreshadowed in the final days June 2013, when interest rates experienced a small spike and the prices of virtually all "safe assets," such as treasuries, mortgage REITs, and long-duration bonds collapsed in the markets.

This analysis does not require a PhD in economics to figure out. Over the long term, we have a pretty good sense of expected ranges of performance from each asset class. Thanks to a whole host of technology solutions, one can simulate thousands of different market scenarios, allowing us to gauge just how far from historic norms we may be in any particular asset class.

It may take a while, but the landscape inevitably shifts, and there will always be a reversion to the historic mean. Bonds will come back to earth. Going forward, investors cannot approach fixed income as they have the last thirty years, and alternative solutions must be approached. However, it is not just fixed income. In general, only by being truly diversified across the breadth of asset classes, such as real assets, credit, and private equity, can we shield ourselves from the fallout of those inevitable shifts.

Risk Diversification

Besides asset types, there are a few other components of best-practice diversification. While almost everyone is familiar with the concept of diversification, remarkably few are familiar with what it means to hedge out or handicap their risks. True diversification isn't simply having an abstract basket of assets. It requires offsetting risks that you have exposure to, investing in negatively correlated assets, and/or employing various forms of hedges.

Virtually every investor that is a homeowner will have insurance against floods, fire, theft, and a whole slew of other potential harms. Yet these very same individuals rarely succeed in insuring what may be the largest portion of their estate—their investable assets—through intelligent risk protection against currency devaluation, interest rate hikes, inflation, or any number of other unexpected scenarios.

Manager Diversification

> **Position Size Policies**
>
> - 1% = Concentrated bet: an investment with a potentially binary outcome (e.g., a single real estate property)
> - 1.5% = Half position: a potentially interesting and appropriate but relatively obscure, strategy (e.g., capital structure arbitrage)
> - 3% = Full position: an investment with a concrete purpose for the portfolio (e.g., an investment with a good mortgage/credit manager)
> - 5–7% = Core position: one of the central drivers of return and protection for the portfolio (e.g., portfolio of global infrastructure assets)
> - 15% = Max. concentration: the maximum exposure an investor should have to any one investment manager or financial institution

Aside from asset classes and risks, the IPS must also include manager diversification guidelines. These guidelines spell out how diversified you will be across individual investment managers and individual positions.

As we have seen with the likes of Lehman, Bear Stearns, Merrill Lynch, Washington Mutual, and Wachovia, no financial institution is too big to fail. Even giants like Citigroup and AIG barely made it off life support in the aftermath of the global financial crisis. And if no one is too big to fail, having too much exposure with any one financial institution may pose an unnecessary risk to a portfolio and be unwise for capital preservation.

To remedy this concern, position sizing becomes a very important risk management strategy. Investing is the exchange of return for risk, and investing comes with the prospect of taking losses. We can, however, control how large and painful those losses may be. This is dictated by the size range of investment positions, and it should be explicitly outlined in the IPS. In my opinion, anything less than 1.5 percent of a portfolio is a position* that is probably not worth taking.

---

* A "position" refers to any single investment. This could be an investment in a particular hedge fund, a piece of real estate, a mortgage, a pool of stocks, or anything else with a specific purpose of function.

Conversely, anything over 5 percent may be too aggressive for those in preservation mode. Also, it is best to limit exposure to 15 percent per financial institution. Assuming an average of 3 percent per position, then, this would require a fully allocated portfolio to have somewhere in range of twenty-five to thirty-five positions with no single institution holding more than five of those positions. This, as you can imagine, takes a great deal of work to find, access, and monitor responsibly.

Geographic Diversification

Aside from asset class diversification and manager diversification, there is also geographic diversification to consider. There are two important factors with geographic considerations. These two factors are, to some extent, mutually exclusive but should be kept in mind nonetheless.

One of the reasons geographic diversification is important is because of *home bias*. This refers to the tendency for most private investors* to invest a disproportionate amount of their net worth in native assets or equity. Investors tend to do this for at least three different reasons.

1. **People take comfort in investing in companies or assets they recognize and can see, feel, and touch.** This is evident from the fact that Canadians keep a large portion of their equities in Canadian markets despite Canada making up less than 3 percent of global GDP. Even more dramatic examples include such countries as New Zealand where locals keep 75 percent in domestic equities despite Kiwi stocks totaling less than 1 percent of the world's total.[23] Among the most home-biased nations are our bankrupt friends the Greeks, whose

---

* I specifically reference private investors, as several studies suggest that institutional investors or sophisticated investors are less prone to a *home bias*.

stocks comprise less than 1 percent of the global economy but constitute 93 percent of their investments.[24] The risk of submitting to a home bias was and is being experienced by Japanese investors. It is estimated that in the early 1990s, as much as 98 percent of Japanese investors' portfolios concentrated on Japanese stocks.[25] Those poor souls who had this allocation at the end of Nikkei's 1989 peak would have then experienced a sustained drawdown of over 80 percent on their portfolios, which has not been recouped in the twenty-plus years since.

2. **Investors believe that domestic opportunities will provide higher returns.** A fascinating study was conducted simultaneously on both German and US investors where both were asked how each country's market would fare relative to the other. German investors expected their stock market to outperform the US market by 2–4 percent per annum. At the same time, US investors expected the Dow Jones to outperform the German index by the exact same margin.[26] And, of course, neither was right.

3. **Investors are afraid of the unknown.** Peter Kenning, a professor at Germany's University of Münster, demonstrated that the mere thought of putting money in foreign or unfamiliar stocks actually generates an automatic sense of discomfort and triggered activity in the amygdala, sending fear throughout the investor's body.[27]

In essence, investing in foreign lands or foreign assets is uncomfortable. As the expression goes, "Everyone wants to go to heaven, but no one wants to die." Without drawing any parallels between foreign assets and one's demise, the same principle applies. Everyone wants to be diversified, but few are prepared to do what it takes to make it happen.

The flip side of home bias is that deliberate geographic diversification is becoming less and less necessary. As our world flattens and companies become truly multinational, a company sitting on the German stock exchange but having China as its largest market will have much more exposure to the Chinese economy than it will to Germany's. In the same vein, according to S&P Dow Jones Indices, at least half of the revenues generated by the S&P 500 today come from outside North America. Expectations are for this number to continue climbing upward, creating implicit geographic diversification within a historically North American index.

In addition, some native indices may actually serve as interesting proxies for other market exposure and provide a much simpler solution for geographic diversification. For example, for a variety of reasons, the Toronto Stock Exchange (TSX), Canada's largest exchange, has a nearly perfect correlation between the domestic benchmark and the MSCI Emerging Markets Index.[28] This means, however, that having exposure to both the TSX and Emerging Markets may create some redundancies in a portfolio, at least from a volatility point of view. Thus, a proper investment plan must strike a balance between avoiding a home bias and avoiding redundancies of geographic diversification.

In summary, we have discussed diversification across asset classes, risks, managers, and geographies. Some might argue that all these measures are exceedingly cautious. I would counter that, much like Pascal's wager,* the potential downside for avoiding this precaution is much greater than the cost of doing the work. Fortunes have been lost due to each of these concentrations, so with the help of capable advisors, investors would be best served avoiding the possibility.

---

* The "wager" is based on the premise that each of us takes on a bet with our lives on the side of God existing (believers) or not existing (atheists). If after one's demise the believer wins, he or she will achieve heaven and have made a limited sacrifice for it (i.e., some prohibited earthly pleasures). If there is no God, he or she loses nothing but these limited sacrifices. However, if the atheist is wrong, that individual has gambled eternal damnation on short-lived pleasures. According to Pascal's analysis, given the opportunity costs, a rational person should live as a believer.

Step Four: Monitoring Plan

The monitoring plan portion of the IPS should spell out exactly when and perhaps even how to review and evaluate the ongoing performance of individual investments and the portfolio as a whole.

The IPS should include how the assets will be evaluated, how often, which benchmarks the assets will be compared to, who will assist in the process (e.g., an investment consultant), and what role they will play. Lastly, it should include just how often the IPS itself will be reviewed to ensure that the circumstances that led to the development of this plan have not changed, requiring the plan itself to be reconsidered. We will delve deeper into how best-practice monitoring can be achieved in the "Managing" section ahead.

Final Caveats on Investment Policy Statements

It is important to distinguish between a tailor-made IPS, which truly accounts for the needs of the investor, and a computer-generated one. Today, more and more financial institutions and advisors are providing their high-net-worth clients with an IPS at the commencement of their working relationship. Unfortunately, these are rarely worth the paper they are printed on. In fact, IPSs created in thirty minutes or through a multiple-choice questionnaire are probably useless. They are more likely menus of the financial institution's offerings than an actionable and meaningful investment plan. They are also often limited to a few asset classes and are thus profoundly insufficient to properly diversify investors.

It is important to constantly remind oneself that the goal of the IPS is not to beat the market. Jason Zweig was reminded of this when he was interviewing the residents of Boca Raton, one of Florida's most affluent retirement communities.

> *Amid the elegant stucco homes, the manicured lawns, the swaying palm trees, the sun and the sea breezes, I asked these folks—mostly in their seventies—if they'd beaten the market over the course of*

their investing lifetimes. Some said yes, some said no. Then one man said, "Who cares? All I know is my investments earned enough for me to end up in Boca."[29]

The goal of an IPS is take charge of one's investment destiny by determining appropriate objectives, developing sound policies, identifying the assets that will get you there, and then holding advisors, money managers, and even yourself accountable.

SOURCING AND SELECTING

Now that you have developed your IPS to guide you, you can start exploring the process of implementation. By selecting the asset classes, you have narrowed down the domains, but you have yet to make the wisest and best-fitting decisions. In much the same way, if you were in the market for a new car, you may have just decided to buy a four-cylinder sedan but still need to determine which make or model is right for you.

Now the shopping begins. This step is not an effortless task. It requires exploring all the options, having extreme patience, getting educated on all the moving parts, and making intelligent decisions. Would you ever consider buying a car without exploring and comparing the options of various makes, models, and manufacturers? Investment selection is no different.

Intelligently sourcing and selecting investments requires reviewing a myriad of options within each asset or sub-asset class, developing a firm grasp of that asset class's universe, and making a decision that is right for you.

Proactive versus Reactive Investing

Most advisors, just like most investors—even sophisticated ones—respond to opportunities that come to them as opposed to proactively searching out those that are best in class. The amazing thing is that many of these investors are former entrepreneurs, and they would never have operated their businesses that way. If they had a piece of software or piece of machinery to buy, they would survey the universe of those that offer that software or machinery and choose the best-fitting solution. In the process of building a successful enterprise, virtually all entrepreneurs have to focus on how they, or their purchasing departments, buy and source. Now that they are successful, however, it seems many have forgotten this important activity, almost expecting good opportunities to show up at their doorstep. But why should sourcing investments be treated any differently from sourcing software or machinery?

Imagine for a moment that an individual is standing in a courtroom on trial for murder. The prosecutor commences the hearing and comes laden with a thirty-slide presentation, filled with all sorts of information that implicates the accused and makes a compelling case for his or her culpability. After the impassioned presentation, the judge is still not fully convinced, so he or she fires back a series of questions. After a number of satisfactory responses from the prosecutor, and without giving so much as a word to the defense or the jury, the judge proclaims the verdict: guilty as charged.

The reaction would be outrageous. In what developed country would this be considered due process? No legal system in the Western world would allow a judgment to be passed without a presentation from the defense, assuring that both sides of the argument be heard. But when it comes to investing, this is exactly how many investors respond. Someone walks into your office pitching a fund, a real estate opportunity, a private equity deal, or any other form of investment accompanied by a PowerPoint presentation. The potential investor will hear it, read it, raise questions or concerns, and then have the presenter of the opportunity address those concerns. After exhausting all the issues or concerns that come to mind, the investor is left with the decision of yea or nay, effectively serving as the judge and jury on the opportunity without ever hearing the defense.

In the courtroom, both the prosecution and the defense are there to protect individuals, as they give the judge and jury an opportunity to holistically assess the facts. Investing is no different. The primary job of an objective advisor is to effectively serve as the devil's advocate in order to avoid investment mistakes.

The bottom line is it is prudent to avoid being reactive to opportunities. In almost every endeavor—in life and in business—results are superior when one goes out to research and proactively identify a best-fitting solution rather than merely responding to what shows up at the door. This is especially true in investing. Thus, it is vital that whoever is advising you fully understands the landscape.

Knowing the Landscape

In 1970, economist George Akerlof wrote a paper entitled, "The Market for Lemons: Quality Uncertainty and the Market Mechanism." In this paper, he outlined the acute problems that negatively impact markets due to asymmetric information. Using the paradigm of used cars, he showed that by virtue of asymmetrical information (i.e., the buyer not being as knowledgeable as the seller), the standard of all the products in the market deteriorates.* There is hardly an area where this is truer than in financial services, where those presenting or manufacturing the investment vehicles have far better insight into the risks involved. It is therefore imperative that the investor and advisor work together to try to rebalance the industry's asymmetry as best they can.

---

* Economists, insurance experts, risk managers, and statisticians refer to this phenomenon as *adverse selection*. Wherever there is an asymmetry in access to information, inferior products or services are more likely to be selected.

Identifying the Cream of the Crop

Identifying the best-in-class investments is first and foremost about avoiding mediocrity. As a general rule of thumb in investing, if something is not a truly high-conviction opportunity, it is always better to pass.* The goal is to identify assets or opportunities that possess extraordinary value, purchased at an attractive price, and that are extremely likely to increase in value over time.†

Getting to this point requires a healthy dose of education, nuanced experience, and sophistication. An art neophyte might view Andy Warhol's *Green Car Crash* or Claude Monet's *Water Lily Pond* and not want to pay twenty dollars for them at a garage sale, whereas an art connoisseur will know immediately that those two pieces are worth a fortune (i.e., $71.7 million and $80.5 million, respectively). A whiskey novice may trade in a glass of thirty-year fine oak Macallan costing over $1,200 a bottle for a strawberry daiquiri because it tastes better, whereas a connoisseur will appreciate the nuances and detect value. Similarly, an experienced advisor can spot opportunities that sit at the apex of investment offerings, knowing exactly where and how to access them.

At the heart of identifying the cream of the crop is the context. When approached with a long-short equity strategy that achieves 9 percent per annum or a first mortgage that projects 7.5 percent per annum, how can you know what is an all-star opportunity or just an average one? The difference between a good and a great opportunity may be just one hundred or two hundred basis points or simply more favorable terms in the offering memorandum. This difference, however,

---

* Investors often do not understand what mediocrity looks like. And more often than not, a seemingly mediocre investment is in fact a supremely inferior one. Without a strong grasp on the range of opportunities, it is best to err on the side of investing only in opportunities that are uniquely and extremely compelling.
† This is true regardless of whether or not its value is currently recognized by the majority of the outside world.

can provide meaningful protection for investors. It allows them to be somewhat wrong and still make a profit. Identifying opportunities that have a sizeable margin of safety is not easy and therefore achieved by few.

The difference between a Hall of Famer and a forgotten baseball player is just one extra hit in every twelve at-bats (i.e., the difference between .333 and a .250 batting average). The difference between an Olympic gold medalist and a last-place finish is often a matter of seconds. Similarly, in investing, a mediocre opportunity might seem very close to an exceptional one, and knowing which is which requires an ability to understand the nuances of excellence.

This is especially true in non-traditional asset classes, or what are often referred to as alternative investments. Research has shown that there are much wider dispersions of returns in non-traditional asset classes than in traditional asset classes. For example, the top-quartile *private* equity funds far outpace the top-quartile *public* equity funds. In the same vein, bottom-quartile private equity managers will have profoundly poorer results than bottom-quartile public equity managers.[30]

Someone with a proven track record of picking talented (i.e., top-quartile) investment managers or opportunities should be able to do so in non-traditional and less efficient asset classes where the pay-off is richer. However, as wider dispersions create greater potential for permanent loss, if an investor cannot find a best-in-class manager or does not have a high-conviction opportunity in this space, it is better to hold on to the cash.

The last thing to know about making good choices is that there is almost no such thing as a best-in-class financial conglomerate. No matter how well renowned the brand, opportunities and funds need to be considered on an individual basis—strategy by strategy, portfolio manager by portfolio manager. Most large financial institutions or banks are a blend of numerous business lines and products. An analogy can be made to whiskey where there is a profound difference between blends and single malts. Blended whiskies are fusions of different whiskies from different distilleries. In contrast, a single-malt is a product of one distillery, where you can identify its origin, the cask it matured in, its age, and have the ability to compare or contrast it with its peers. That is why while some 90 percent of whiskies that are consumed globally are blends, over 95 percent of the whiskies that are sold at auctions and go for significant premiums are single malts.[31] Thus despite investors having a relationship with one or two large institutions, that dynamic is unlikely to ensure that one is accessing best-in-class opportunities in every asset class. The products from these large financial institutions will be varied and extensive, but they are certainly not all exceptional. Some may be great, and some may be terrible. Focusing on individual money managers, however, irrespective of which institution they hail from, allows one to identify those who are among the best in executing their investment strategy with the ability to outperform their peers over time.

Having Options

From the day they are born, children have a proliferation of synapses in the brain. Until the age of three, more and more synaptic connections are formed each day. A toddler is estimated to have as many as a quadrillion synaptic connections, more than double as many as adults. This allows children to be more flexible and adaptable than adults.[32]

What follows in the years ahead is referred to as the process of Hebbian learning. As the child continues growing, the synaptic connections that they employ in their daily lives are strengthened, and those that they do not use get pruned.[33] It is estimated that children proceed to lose as many as twenty billion synaptic connections each day.[34] Michael Mauboussin points out that this process refines the brain, allowing it to survive and thrive in the specific environments in which we find ourselves. In *More Than You Know*, Michael Mauboussin explains:

When the environment is uncertain, it helps to start with lots of alternatives (e.g. synaptic connections) and then select (via pruning) the ones that are best given the environment. The process is undoubtedly costly because lots of energy and resources necessarily go to waste, but it's the best one going.[35]

This biological insight provides an equally significant message for both investors and advisors. Besides knowing about the best-in-class opportunities and having access to them, one must have a sufficient number of comparable alternatives from which to prune in order to make wise investment decisions.

In *Smart Choices: A Practical Guide to Making Better Life Decisions*, three management consultant gurus, John S. Hammond, Ralph L. Keeney, and Howard Raiffa, outline their view about how a good decision-making process should take place. They write that instead of using gut decisions, default options, or limited opportunity sets, individuals should always actively search out the best options or alternatives. Only then can they determine which best meet their objectives and proceed accordingly.

In deciding to remodel your kitchen, you would solicit proposals from several contractors and then review the quotes line by line, making sure you understood everything before hiring someone to come into your home because this has a direct and intimate impact on your life. Although investing is not the same as having a carpenter in your breakfast nook in the morning, it should be approached the same; all options or alternatives should be considered before making a decision. Investors, however, have a tendency to select their first option, the default option, or some other reactive approach. This is true in the selection of advisors and the selection of investments. Investors may use an advisor from their community, participate in a real estate deal brought to them by their cousin, or invest in the business of a friend. Unfortunately, it is precisely this type of decision-making that leads people down the path of investing in mediocrity and away from the path of preservation.

It is somewhat intuitive that more options are better than none, but the extent to which that is true may be shocking. In a study of Fortune 500 senior executives, it was found that when executives considered more than one alternative, they made six times as many very good decisions (as opposed to those they rated "satisfactory" or "poor").[36]

In his notable work *The Most Important Thing: Uncommon Sense for the Thoughtful Investor*, Howard Marks writes:

> *Investment is a discipline of relative selection... First the process of investing has to be rigorous and disciplined. Second, it is by necessity comparative. Whether prices are depressed or elevated, and whether prospective returns are therefore high or low, we have to find the best investments out there. Since we can't change the market, if we want to participate, our only option is to select the best from the possibilities that exist. These are relative decisions.[37]*

This approach stands in stark contrast to the practice of large financial institutions, banks, and brokerage houses that manage to deploy 100 percent of the capital as soon as it walks through the door. This speed is a telltale sign of poor capital allocation. Relative selection and sourcing the best in class requires time and that one indispensable attribute in investing: patience.

Patience

Historians suggest that for most of human history, we occupied ourselves with two central activities: hunting and gathering. And somewhere between 30,000 BCE and 10,000 BCE, we learned how to cultivate crops and domesticate animals, and gradually we evolved into farmers. This evolution into a higher order is characterized by patience, patience to wait and see what happens to the seed that drops in the ground and patience to see what will happen if small changes are made to the growth of that seed in the next season.

Patience has served us well in our evolution. Farming allowed us to maximize our food production and achieve some certainty about where the next meal would come from. But our hunter-gatherer instinct has not left us completely. In our past lives, quick reactions were imperative. Deliberations and contemplations simply didn't serve you well if a tiger or bear was closing in or if some other animal was waiting to eat that fruit ripening on the tree. Waiting might mean death or at least an empty stomach. In these circumstances, patience and thoughtfulness were not required or even desired traits;[38] but where there is relative safety and subsistence, patience and thoughtfulness become necessary traits to preserve what we have.

There is no better sport of patience than baseball. Warren Buffett is often quoted on his advice to "wait for a fat pitch," meaning that you should avoid pitches (i.e., opportunities) that aren't coming down the middle of the plate and thus positioned as well as possible for success. Buffett famously used this quote in Berkshire Hathaway's 1997 annual report in reference to legendary Hall of Famer Ted Williams.

Williams was one of the greatest hitters in the history of major league baseball, and Buffett claimed that what contributed to Williams's success was his understanding of the sweet spot. Williams apparently broke down the strike zone into seventy-seven different baseball-sized cells. He figured out that his batting average was much better when pitches came into certain specific cells, and he always tried to bat accordingly. As a result of his research, Williams became a nineteen-time All-Star, two-time MVP and Triple-Crown winner, holding the highest career batting average of anyone in the five-hundred-plus home run club.

In investing, the hardest part is taking the time to identify those seventy-seven cells, familiarizing oneself with the opportunity set, and recognizing how to consistently choose from the best options available. This is difficult for two reasons. One, knowing the full range of options is very hard (perhaps even impossible). Two, the hardest part of this process is that these options must be considered simultaneously. For example, having seen twenty-five land development projects over a thirty-year career will be useful, but it is not quite as helpful as having compared those same land development opportunities in a short period of time. A real-time comparison provides the most acute understanding of what a superior deal looks like and helps make better investment decisions.

A famous study conducted at Stanford University compared magazine ad designers working simultaneously and those working sequentially. All other things being equal, the ads that were designed simultaneously proved to be much more effective in achieving their goals than the designs that were done sequentially.[39] Having the luxury of apples-to-apples comparisons in real time will invariably improve our decision-making abilities. But only up to a point. There is a body of research that suggests that more choice actually has the opposite impact. Having too many choices actually reduces the likelihood of making any choice at all, as the chooser tends to fall into a decision paralysis, and if a choice is made, the plethora of choices reduces the satisfaction in the decision. This phenomenon was noted by Barry Schwartz in his 2004 book *The Paradox of Choice: Why More Is Less*. A safeguard against this choice overload, however, comes from having a high level of expertise or well-defined preferences. If a person is very particular about how a cup of coffee or a cocktail is made, for example, more options tend to increase satisfaction.[40] Similarly, a study of Silicon Valley executives found that those presented with more choices in their field of expertise were actually able to make quicker and more efficient decisions.[41]

This nuance of choice overload is experienced by everyone, every day, as we are all experts in our own preferences. Take, for example, shopping at a large grocery store. Every time we decide to turn in to an aisle of soft drinks, ice cream, or cereals in a supermarket, we subconsciously enter into expertise mode. In the cereal aisle, I, for example, will slip past the children's cereals. In fact, I pass all sugary cereals on way to my favorite muesli selections. I avoid those with almonds (allergy), and I look for a smaller box because it fits nicely in my cupboard. Even in an unfamiliar store without my usual brand, I can quickly go through my subconscious checklist, looking for the one with high protein and high fiber, one that doesn't get too soggy in milk, not too sweet, but not as bland as chicken feed. If there's a brand I trust, I will go there first. This entire process working almost instantaneously in the background entails hundreds of considerations, remembrances, comparisons, and overlapping decisions, but I have never had a problem choosing a cereal.

In less than a couple of minutes, we can deconstruct product categories and brands, cascade through subcategories and sub-subcategories, and funnel our process down to the dimensions and the most trivial of details to pick the item that best serves our interest. This incredible ability to achieve sophistication is inherent in all of us. Recognizing this capacity, the question must be asked, "What stops us or, more importantly, our advisors, from achieving this same level of sophistication in investing? What interferes with our ability to make quicker, more intelligent investment decisions?"

Good Shoppers versus Good Investors

In 2000, Malcolm Gladwell popularized the term *market maven* in his book *Blink*. In it, he introduces the research of Linda Price and Lawrence Feick on a personality type that is intuitively and instinctively a market maven. These individuals are extraordinary shoppers and passionate gatherers of information, knowing the best prices and all the associated features. They are those people who are often ahead of the trend in their area of interest.[42] Not everyone is a market maven, but everyone can benefit from improved shopping skills; although with that said, to be an effective advisor, shopping is not all that is needed, and good shoppers are not necessarily good planners or strategists.

A market maven can tell you what is priced well and compare every feature of a given product or service. However, he or she is missing many of the most critical elements of investing: the decision-making process. A market maven can tell you where to purchase the creamiest peanut butter but not whether it works with the cookie recipe you are preparing. Many advisors are actually market mavens. They may be exceptionally good shoppers and even understand the intricacies of various investment vehicles, but they lack abilities in the decision-making processes that will safeguard against their clients' human errors, biases, or poor decisions over the long term.

Appropriateness

After determining that an opportunity makes sense, the last and final question to be asked is: *Does this opportunity make sense for me?* If an investor is in need of immediate cash flow and is presented with a real estate construction or development opportunity, there are no terms in the world that could make that opportunity suitable. You may be enamored with a particular broker or money manager, but that doesn't necessarily mean he or she will help you preserve your capital. Someone may be the best real estate manager in the world, but if 90 percent of your portfolio is already in multi-residential assets, investing more with this manager will not be the best diversification option for you.

One of the most important skill sets an advisor must have and an investor can develop is the discipline to know what they will not invest in and learning to be comfortable saying no. This is more difficult than it appears, especially when you can appreciate just how good the investment may be.

Algorithms and Robo-Advisors

Investment selection cannot be replicated with an algorithm, a database, or any other piece of technology alone. There will always be those touting the latest and greatest system, claiming that it could solve all investing problems with the click of a button. The technology of the future may make me eat my words one day, but I believe it is unlikely that the subjective art and science of advising affluent investors—dealing with all their specific wants and needs—can be boiled down to a mathematical formula, algorithm, or line of code any more than a raising a child can be boiled down to a robo-parent singing lullabies. There are too many human elements that simply cannot be quantified.

Even if we put the advisory element aside, there is no concrete evidence that algorithmic trading can produce consistent outperformance over the long run.[43] In fact, Nobel Prize–winning economist Eugene Fama claims that one of his earliest revelations about the markets came during his last year as an undergraduate student at Tufts University. While working for economics professor Harry Ernst, who also had a stock market forecasting service, Fama was given the responsibility of inventing trading strategies and algorithms to forecast the market. In his efforts, he found numerous formulas that beat the market when back-tested but when put to the test in real life were practically useless.[44] He found that markets, at least in the short to medium term, are inherently unpredictable.

Fama's experience puts into question all the newsletter marketers who claim that if by subscribing to their stock picks, investors would have yielded consistent triple-digit returns that exceeded the success of investor legends like Warren Buffett and George Soros by a factor of five.[45] It could be that these assertions are always in the past tense. It seems subscribers always just missed out on that return rate.*

---

* Notably, none of these individuals can be found on the Forbes Billionaires List. Compounding at their rate of return should have certainly gotten them there.

This reality is illustrated in the writings of Murray Stahl. In *Collected Commentaries and Conundrums Regarding Value Investing*, Stahl shares a fascinating study where a group of finance gurus were challenged to create a singular model that could have been used (with the benefit of hindsight) to predict the top-performing stocks of the last fifty years.[46] Not one person could produce a model that had the capacity to select the top ten stocks of the last half century. If it is so difficult to create a model that simply reproduced the performance of the known past, how likely is it that another model or algorithm would be effective in making decisions about the future?

RESEARCHING

With asset classes decided upon and an understanding of the options available, there is only one last step before making an investment decision: proper due diligence. This may seem like a clear need, but the unfortunate reality is that the critical task of due diligence rarely gets the time and attention it deserves. Indeed, this step is truly what separates top-tier advisors from the rest.

Many professions must follow structured, repeatable processes that define their ability to excel. Pilots, for example, are required to go through a set of detailed, predetermined steps every time they enter the cockpit. The bigger the risk, the more checklists and due diligence are required. Hospitals are ripe with them: nurses check and double-check everything from patient name to temperature, and surgeons triple-check basics, such as asking the patient to repeat his or her name and date of birth, before suiting up. These sometimes tedious tasks are the very foundation of excellence, but investment management has largely avoided this type of discipline. As a result, far too many investment managers and advisors expose their clients' money to risks by making careless mistakes as a result of a lack of due diligence. It may not be the same as putting your life in the hands of a pilot or surgeon, but investing is just as much a complicated, high-stakes, and emotion-laden profession. Without a defined process, people can easily lose their way.

One of the most important medical discoveries of the last 150 years in terms of lives saved is handwashing. In 1847, Ignaz Semmelweis discovered that this simple act could reduce the spread of infection and bring down the mortality rate of puerperal fever following childbirth from 35 percent to under 1 percent. However, as shocking as it sounds to us today, Semmelweis's findings were not accepted by his peers, and he was dismissed from his hospital. Today, not only is handwashing a lifesaver, it has been added to the foundational checklist of every surgeon, who would not think of picking up an instrument until hands and forearms had been soaped and rinsed and sanitized.

Many seasoned investors and veteran investment professionals may discount the simplicity of checklists, claiming that they know what to look for, that they can follow their gut, or that they can do the analysis in their sleep. This may be true at certain times and on certain days, but checklists are there to protect us from ourselves.

Some investment professionals may see checklists as tedious or unnecessary, but there is a brilliance to them. They allow investment research to be approached the same way as a trip to the grocery store (and who has not returned home only to realize he or she forgot to buy the milk?). Virtually every investment could be subject to the same set of basic, yet profoundly important, questions. Such checklist investing may seem overly artless and unsophisticated, but it is an integral part of successful investing.

When advisors and investors use a checklist of standardized questions to approach every investment situation, they eliminate the chance of missing the big picture. They are forced to consider every single investment opportunity from every single angle, even if it seems like a waste of time on the surface.

Almost all investments worthy of consideration have a number of moving parts. To subject oneself to the risk of each part without probing the specifics would seem irresponsible in any environment. Imagine planning out your week without looking at what is already on your calendar or putting together new furniture without looking at the instructions beforehand. You could do it, but you are taking a chance that you will miss something. In investing, where the stakes are so high, checklists that clarify the various moving parts are an important part of the process.

Although checklists are used for some of the highest-trained professions with the highest stakes (e.g., doctors, engineers, pilots), investment advisors seem to take the idea as a personal slight (much as those doctors did for handwashing). Using a checklist to make high-level decisions does require humility. It suggests the possibility of error, which many find bruising to the ego, and having one's professional responsibilities distilled into a list can seem demeaning to a skilled professional. But this perspective is damaging. The truth is that many people are able to form an opinion about what is in front of them, but few can see what is not there but should be. Checklists allow you to avoid these oversights.

Inherent in checklists is a willingness and commitment to adopt investment discipline. The word *discipline* does not generally excite people, but discipline is what is needed to suspend our egos and infuse the process with the intellectual honesty it deserves. Part of this discipline is a willingness to be transparent, or honest, about your needs and gaps in knowledge, and a willingness to work with teams. Many advisors operate without communicating with others, preferring to be the white knight for their clients. Similarly, many investors are uncomfortable with collaboration, as they are sensitive about their wealth. However, proper due diligence for the advisor and the investor necessitates them to step outside of their comfort zone and engage with others. Checklists will often require us to pick up the phone, make inquiries, and conduct on-site visits and interviews.

These values—discipline, transparency, and teamwork—are absent in many professions. It requires an awareness of one's limitations and humbleness. However, to have discipline and to embrace transparency and teamwork will bring benefits to the investor and his or her portfolio that are more than worth the effort.

Investment Checklists

At my firm, we use at least four different checklists, which are part of our four-step investment process. These checklists allow us to thoroughly complete the operational, qualitative, and quantitative due diligence. We may still make mistakes, but with this process the likelihood of them is profoundly diminished.

Here is a short summary of the four-step process we follow:

The Initial Screen *(Checklist #1)*

We come across dozens of new opportunities each week. This translates into several thousand opportunities each year. Considering that more than 90 percent of the opportunities out there are not worth the paper they are written on, it would not be logical or economical to research all of them. To help us make quick decisions, we employ an investment sieve that requires no more than ten or fifteen minutes to complete. We refer to this as *the initial screen.*

The initial screen that we employ is a pass/fail test. The questions are in a simple yes/no format to see if an opportunity meets our minimum criteria. We are not looking to make an investment decision at this point, so we gather just enough information to separate the wheat from the chaff. It is important to note that different asset classes and investments will have different types of screens. The graph provides a sampling of questions that may appear on one such initial screen.*

---

* Please note that this screen is specifically relevant for well-heeled hedge funds and seasoned investment managers, not emerging/start-up managers, opportunistic funds, private equity or real assets. Each requires an entirely different screen.

CRITERIA	SAMPLE SCREEN QUESTIONS
Interests Alignment	Is the management fee strategy average or better?
	Is there a perpetual high watermark?
	Does the manager have a significant percentage of personal assets invested in the fund, opportunity, or strategy?
Investment Process	Is the track record of past performance third-party verified?
	Does it meet our minimum required return for the given strategy?
	Does management have a consistent investment philosophy (i.e., avoiding trying to be all things to all people)?
	Does the manager have an identifiable edge (e.g., depth of analysis, time horizon, infrastructure, unique sourcing or market access)?
Market Opportunity	Is the manager operating in a market that shows strong signs of a bubble?
	Is there at least one clearly identifiable source of inefficiency for the market in which the strategy operates (e.g., illiquidity, analytical complexity, informational opacity, market segmentation, low quantity/capacity of capital, excessive fear)?
Organizational Attributes	Are the liquidity terms reasonable given the investment horizon and liquidity level of underlying securities?
	If the manager has more than one product, do the different strategies employed have one underlying specialization?
	Is the manager willing and able to provide sufficient materials and documentation for due diligence?
	Are all the third parties involved (e.g., auditor, administrator, custodian) reputable and verifiable?

The Research Report *(Checklist #2)*

If an opportunity passes the initial screen, what follows is a more comprehensive checklist, the complete research report. Calling this report a checklist actually trivializes how deep and thorough this analysis actually is and needs to be, but for consistency's sake, we will work with the terminology.

In my firm, the report we prepare when conducting our due diligence generally focuses on ten key categories. These categories are

1) Investment Manager—Compensation
2) Investment Manager—Co-investment
3) Investment Manager—Ethics
4) Investment Manager—Capability
5) Investment Strategy—Understandability
6) Investment Strategy—Risk Management
7) Competitive Advantage
8) Market Opportunity
9) Organizational Liquidity and Capacity
10) Asset Valuation

Each of these categories includes more specific questions. As the questions have a high standard, no investment scores perfectly on all of them; however, if enough of the questions get acceptable answers and the whole picture makes sense, then there is reason to consider the opportunity. This is just one way of avoiding the pitfall of myopia, focusing on just one small part of the puzzle and losing sight of the forest for the trees.

The Manager Interview and Background Check (Checklist #3)

Once the research report has been completed, we want to get to know the people involved. This involves an interview along with a site visit to ensure that all the key players (especially those executing the trades) are known and provide us with a level of comfort.

After we have met the team members and found them impressive, there is only one way to test our impressions. Check with the people who have known them well and have worked with them in the past. This includes references the team members provided and references that they did not volunteer.*

By the time we are speaking with references, we have all the technical information we need about the opportunity. The purpose of this exercise is to verify the integrity, decency, and moral standing of the people involved, which should confirm our initial positive impressions. To receive a sampling of manager interview and reference check questions, feel free to e-mail me at mo@primequadrant.com. We always tailor these questions to the investment manager or strategy, but the sample will give you a sense of what we might look for.

Investment Committee Meeting (Checklist #4)

If the screen, research report, interview, site visit, and references have all met or exceeded our standards, there is one last step in the process. This step ensures that several eyes and minds have had the chance to comment on the opportunity. This stage involves a meeting with the investment committee† and encourages everyone to

---

* To give you a sense of how important this is, I can tell you that we have never participated in a deal or invested in a fund that didn't meet this criteria.
† Everyone should have an investment committee, whether it's an advisor, a family member, or anyone else who can bring another perspective to the table.

play devil's advocate and ask open-ended questions, such as "Are we missing anything here?" "Have we slipped up in this realm before?" or "Are we comfortable with our findings?"

Keep It Simple

These processes may sound tedious, onerous, and even overwhelming. The reality is that they absolutely are tedious, and most investors will not have the determination or desire to see it through. That is why most investors invest rather poorly (even if they don't realize it) and why research and consulting firms exist; to help investors delegate what they are unwilling, unable, or uninterested in doing themselves.

There are, however, four basic questions that investors must be able to answer themselves. In a way, these four questions can serve as a summary for everything I've said thus far.

1. Am I dealing with good people?

Warren Buffett said, "We've never succeeded in making a good deal with a bad person … I learned to only go into business with people who I like, trust, and admire." Note that Buffett was not talking about which university someone attended or which Wall Street darling he or she worked at or with. He is asking a very simple question: "How do I feel about this person?" To get a good feel for people, you need to look behind the glossy marketing brochure and ask first and foremost whether you are dealing with individuals of integrity. A quick way to gauge this is to watch how they treat subordinates or those they do not need to curry favor from. Of course, you should make sure they possess the appropriate skill sets for the opportunity, but above all you want to know if they are likable, trustworthy, and admirable.

2. How do I make money?

After discerning that the investment opportunity comes from some-one you want to deal with, you need to determine whether the strat-egy is logical and if it makes sense to you. Is there a definitive edge? Can the business be commoditized in a context where it's hard to be smarter than the most simple-minded competitor? Why does this opportunity exist? Is there a dislocation that warrants it? What are the constraints of this space? How does this fit within broader market conditions? If the money-making strategy, or any element of it, does not make perfect sense to you, hold off investing until it does.

3. How do I not lose money?

Although an opportunity may be compelling, it's important to under-stand the risks involved. Are the risks knowable? Are they controll-able? Which ones are you getting paid for, and which ones are you not getting paid for? Are there operational risks that can put your money at risk? What happens if the market takes a drastic move in a particular direction? And if it does go down in market price, would you want to buy more of it? Is there agency risk?* What is the worst-case scenario, and how could it be mitigated? These are just a few of the questions you'll want to ask yourself to be sure you are knowl-edgeable and comfortable with the risks involved. If you cannot do this level of analysis yourself, make sure that your advisor does it and provides you with a summary thereof.

---

* Agency risk is the risk that the agents of the investment (i.e., the managers) will use the opportunity to benefit themselves rather than the investor. For example, the man-ager may decide to self-servingly increase overhead costs rather than distribute the extra profits to investors or elect to take greater risk than the investor would be com-fortable with because it might result in a higher payoff to the manager.

4. Is this opportunity right for me?

Even after getting comfortable with all of the above, you still have to ask yourself whether or not the opportunity is appropriate for you. Will it further diversify your portfolio or will it add concentration? Might it cause you excessive anxiety or compromise your well-being? Does it violate any of your values or personal beliefs? How does it fit into your overall IPS, considering both your short-term and long-term goals?

It may seem like a bit of work (and it is), but if you can confidently answer each of these four questions for every opportunity you participate in, you will sleep better at night and make wiser investment decisions along the way.

MANAGING

Seeing the Big Picture

There is an old anecdote about several blind men in a room with an elephant. One man holds the elephant's tail and thinks it is a snake. Another man touches the elephant's leg and thinks it is a tree trunk. All the men hold one part of the elephant and think it is something else because they cannot put the big picture together.

The elephant problem is one of the most pervasive issues that face private investors. Every investment product that is sold to people has one aspect—a tail, a leg, or a trunk—that looks enticing. Maybe the investment has a high cash yield and you want current income. Maybe the investment has a great story behind it, such as the emerging middle class in a developing country. Or maybe it is just being sold to you by someone you like as a person. These factors may be important in isolation, but it is much more important to see the whole picture and analyze each investment opportunity in its entirety.

One classic and grave example of the elephant problem in recent history relates to mortgage-backed securities, the investments at the center of the financial crisis in 2008. Even sophisticated investors, such as pension plans, banks, and insurance companies, bought these securities by the armful. One of the main reasons for this rapacious purchasing was that one part of the whole picture was very compelling: these securities had the highest credit rating in the market but offered a better return than government bonds. What a bargain!

As Warren Buffett has often said, "When the tide goes out, that's when you learn who's been swimming naked." In this case, the tide went out during the financial crisis and these investors, who focused on something in isolation instead of the big picture, were left exposed to permanent and devastating losses.

The financial crisis is an extreme example, but it shows how important it is to try to see the big picture. Responsible stewards of capital need to have the ability to piece together the big picture—by asking questions and working with others—and make decisions accordingly. To do this properly, investors must employ advisors or consultants who have the humility and expertise to ask the right questions and be capable of seeing the bigger picture

The need for a larger perspective applies not only to specific investments but to the whole portfolio as well. Having different people advising on different segments of a portfolio without seeing the bigger picture is equivalent to having different architects working on different parts of your house. Just consider what your home might look like with all these experts pulling in their own directions; your portfolio would be no different.

Monitor the Portfolio

Monitoring the portfolio generally includes two types of monitoring functions:

- Monitoring the work that others are doing for you (e.g., investment managers, brokers, and service providers)
- Monitoring the impact of our world on your portfolio (e.g., current events, trends, and market dynamics)

In monitoring those doing the work, you are essentially ensuring the investment managers are doing what they said they were going to do and addressing issues as they surface (e.g., style drift). To monitor them, you will need to read their monthly, quarterly, and annual reports, measure performance, and employ proper benchmarks or comparisons. You may also need to monitor administrative changes to the team—ensuring no key person unexpectedly departs—and check that all the service providers (i.e., administrators, custodians, and auditors) are still in place.

On a quarterly basis, manager performance should be reviewed and benchmarked against stated objectives and/or peer performances. On an annual basis, the risk tolerance, investment objectives, and the entire IPS should be reviewed. While slightly more involvement may be beneficial, reviewing the market value of one's investments more than once a month is actually ill-advised. Too much monitoring, especially for assets in the public markets, could prompt some very unhealthy investor behaviors. A common example of this is overreacting to routine volatility where not acting would have been preferred. This is harder than it seems. Having a consultant or a trusted advisor who won't fuel that bias by trying to sell you a new product can help you stay true to the process and avoid costly mistakes.

At all times, it helps to read all the associated reports and letters provided by the various investment managers or advisors holding the assets. Investors should ask questions and be committed to continuous learning. At the very least, one should be on the lookout for red flags, such as style drift, lapsed communications, and the relevance of the strategy under global macro conditions.

In monitoring the impact of the world around you, you want to ensure that you are diligently managing the cash levels, as well as general liquidity, currency, and interest rate exposure. This form of monitoring would also include reviewing the asset allocation and assessing the go-forward prospects for specific asset classes. When markets are booming and certain asset classes have spiked, this exercise should prompt you to take money (and risk) off the table. Similarly, in times of market turmoil, this will allow you to buy those investments that have become very cheap. This is central to the disciplined regiment of rebalancing.

Introduction to Rebalancing

The simplest way to understand the progression from monitoring to rebalancing is with an analogy to the annual checkup with your doctor. There is hardly anything more basic than the need for an annual checkup where one could see if everything is status quo or if there has been an unexpected deviation (e.g., blood sugar levels too low, cholesterol too high, unusual weight gain or loss). These checkups provide the patient with the opportunity to spot – i.e. monitor - any problem or deviation from the norm and correct – i.e. rebalance - it.

Those who skip a year or two are often urged (or perhaps dragged) by their loved ones to make that checkup. Yet, notwithstanding these good habits with our physical health, most investors have not adopted them in their financial health. It is simply remarkable that investors can go such long periods of time, possibly even a lifetime, without ever considering a checkup to rebalance their portfolio. In 1986, there was a study conducted on the investment habits of the 850,000 individuals employed in higher education. The remarkable thing is that over their entire investment lifetime, more than 72 percent of these individuals never made a single change to their asset allocation mix, and fewer than 2.5 percent made a change in any given year. Most simply held on to the same funds they bought on day one without making any changes whatsoever.[47] This is consistent with another study demonstrating that nearly 80 percent of the 1.2 million 401(k) investors with retirement accounts didn't move one penny from one fund to another fund in a two-year period where markets rallied over 40 percent.[48]

Investors can be very pleased or dissatisfied with their investments, and they may even be aware of problems, but most rarely go through the efforts of a portfolio checkup or employ the crucial discipline of portfolio rebalancing, which should be done once a year. Portfolio rebalancing shifts the portfolio to adhere to the asset allocation bands outlined in the IPS. For example, when equities take a tumble and fixed income becomes a larger portion of the portfolio, rebalancing may include selling off some of the more expensive fixed-income investments and purchase cheaper equities.

Benjamin Graham, the father of value investing, said, "The essence of investment management is the management of risks, not the management of returns." Unfortunately, investors seldom spend sufficient time determining where heightened risk lies, what can go wrong, where the portfolio is overconcentrated, and what they can do about it. At the heart of this neglect to manage risk is investors' complacency with success, the very condition rebalancing aims to cure.

Complacency

In general, there is a harmful human tendency to become complacent and to maintain the status quo even when matters of greatest significance are on the line. In one study, Eric Johnson and Daniel Goldstein were perplexed by the higher organ donation rates in Austria, Belgium, France, and Hungary as compared to Denmark, the Netherlands, the United Kingdom, and Germany. Nearly 100 percent of automobile drivers in the first group elected to donate their organs, compared to less than 30 percent in the latter group. What they discovered was not a cultural or humanistic difference between the countries but something much simpler. It was the phrasing of the organ donation question on the form.[49] In the latter group, the form had the following statement: "Please check the box below if you would like to participate in the organ donor program." People did not check the box, and they ended up not volunteering to donate their organs. In the former group, the form had the following statement: "Please check the box below if you would *not* like to participate in the organ donor program." Again people did not check the box, but this time they ended up volunteering to donate their organs.

Dan Ariely, author of *Predictably Irrational: The Hidden Forces That Shape Our Decisions*, explains that people did not choose the default position because they were lazy or because the question was unimportant. In fact, it was the exact opposite. People were faced with such an important and complicated issue that in the absence of a clear choice, they reacted by choosing the default option.

In investing, which has its fair share of complexity and innumerable options and opinions, maintaining the status quo is even more tempting. But maintaining the status quo may have painful consequences for the portfolios and lifestyles of investors.

Missing the Chance to Rebalance

After having being recruited by George Soros, Victor Niederhoffer soon found himself managing all of Soros's fixed income and foreign exchange investments. Shortly thereafter, Niederhoffer founded his own fund, which was returning him and his investors 35 percent per annum. In 1996, *Managed Account Reports* ranked Niederhoffer the number-one hedge fund manager in the world. Soros held Niederhoffer in such high regard that when it was time to train Soros Jr. in the theory and practice of investing, George deferred to Victor to serve as his son's mentor.[50] At that time, Niederhoffer claimed to have traded about two million contracts with an average profit of seventy dollars per contract. In case anyone attributes his success to luck, "this average is approximately 700 standard deviations away from randomness."[51]

Five years after closing his first fund in 1997, Niederhoffer opened the Matador Fund and Manchester Trading, predicting short-term market movements. Over the next five years, his fund produced annual returns of 50 percent per year. In 2006, these two funds were awarded by MARHedge for having the best-performing commodity trading advisors. Just one year later, after a few bad bets on subprime mortgages and a 75 percent drawdown, the Matador Fund was closed.

This Harvard-educated legend with financial brilliance who impressed the likes of George Soros and who demonstrated extraordinary investment skill lost investors nearly every dime they had entrusted to him. How could anyone have done better with their manager selection process? And what could investors have done to escape such a miserable fate? The answer is, nothing but the disciplined routine of rebalancing—taking money off the table after significant profits were had.

This is true not just for Niederhoffer but almost any industry star. In *The* Clash *of the Cultures*, Jack Bogle highlights some of the most dramatic reversals in the mutual fund world.[52] A look at his case studies illustrates how common and how dramatic these reversals can be.

Fund	Years of Outperformance	Years of Underperformance
CGM Focus Fund	• 1998–2007, grew asset base to $6 billion • Return of 917 percent vs. 78 percent for the S&P 500	• 2007–2011, the fund lost more than half of its value • S&P lost 6 percent for the same period
The Janus Fund	• 18.5 percent from 1971–1999 • Assets quickly ballooned to $43 billion in 2000	• From 2000, lost 28 percent vs. the 7 percent gains for the S&P 500 • By 2012, roughly 82 percent of the assets from 2000 had departed
Legg Mason Value Trust Fund	• Only mutual fund in history to outpace the S&P 500 for 15 consecutive years	• 2006–2008, the fund had a cumulative loss of over 56 percent • The S&P 500 lost less than half for same period
PBHG Growth Fund	• Cumulative return of 671 percent between 1988 and 1996 • More than doubled the S&P 500s performance	• 1996–1998, a cumulative return of 6 percent versus 64 percent for S&P • 2000–2003, losses of 56 percent tripled the drawdown of the S&P 500
T. Rowe Price Growth Fund	• 1950–1971, exceeded the S&P 500 by over 600 percent	• 1971–1988, the fund's cumulative return of 172 percent vs. 470 percent for the S&P 500
Vanguard US Growth Fund	• 1961–1967, had the best return in the industry • Returned 327 percent versus 108 percent for the S&P 500	• 1968–2012, fund returns ranged from pedestrian to pathetic • 1999–2012, fund lost a cumulative 45 percent versus the 7 percent gain for the S&P 500
The Fidelity Magellan Fund	• 1964–1990, produced annual returns of 22 percent • Double the performance of the S&P 500	• 1990–2011, the S&P 500 outperformed the Magellan Fund by almost the same margin • 2012, the fund's assets fell from over $105 to $15 billion.

While some of these funds have reversed course again and may come to be the darlings of retail investment advisors once again, the point remains. No one prospers and outperforms eternally. Even Berkshire Hathaway will have many years of underperforming the S&P 500. That is a fact, not an opinion. So what are investors to do? The answer lies in the simple exercise of regular and disciplined rebalancing.

Fighting Complacency

A simple way to combat complacency is to ask a simple question: *If I had to recreate my portfolio today, would it look the same?* If the answer is no, it is time to change the portfolio. This is a tactic many Fortune 500 CEOs employ in their companies. When pressed with a difficult situation, shrewd CEOs imagine someone else taking over the company and ask themselves what their successor would do.[53]

The beauty of being an investor is that answering this question does not require a meeting with a board, a memo to compliance, or meetings with human resources or marketing. And any decision can be executed expeditiously, especially with liquid assets.

In military terminology, the acronym VUCA came to connote the general conditions of most battle terrains. Those conditions included volatility (the nature and dynamics of change), uncertainty (the ongoing possibility of the unknowable), complexity (the intertwining of many issues and forces), and ambiguity (the difficult assessment of reality or cause and effect). VUCA may yet be a better description of investing than anything we have said until now, as the only way to approach VUCA is to be aware, to be ready for the unexpected, and to be nimble enough to change when facts on the ground warrant it.

In the realm of public markets, Wall Street analysts frequently reduce their research to one of three actionable decisions: buy, hold, or sell. The problem is one of these is almost irrelevant and meaningless. There should be no "hold" option. The market offers you a price every day, and it is either a good price or it is poor price. It's hardly ever the perfect price and certainly not so for any sustained period of time. Thus, no one should hold investments they wouldn't buy today.* And even with other assets, if you're not selling, you are effectively buying. If you own real estate that jumped several hundred dol-

---

* This may be more difficult with real assets, private equity, and even some types of hedge funds though the same general principal applies.

lars per square foot or a fund that has had its net asset value catapult and you would never buy the same at today's price, then you should consider selling it. Otherwise, acknowledge the fact that you essentially just bought it again.

I am not advocating for investors or even discretionary advisors to be trading securities every time the market moves. That comes at a hefty price (i.e., transaction costs) and is rather unhealthy (e.g., invites too many behavioral biases). I am simply suggesting that investors take a disciplined approach to buying and selling decisions and avoid irrationally forming emotional connections with their investments. Howard Lutnick, the chairman and chief executive officer of Cantor Fitzgerald, describes how often investors describe their holdings as if they are married to them: "You know, back when I bought that stock, things were really good. I paid 10, then it was 12, then 14—the honeymoon was great ... Then things got rough for a while. And now it's 6. But I've married this stock for better or worse, until death do we part so I'm hanging in there."[54]

This phenomenon is something behavioral psychologists have referred to as the endowment effect where value is ascribed to something simply because it is already owned. In one of the most famous studies on the endowment effect, test subjects received mugs as gifts after indicating what they would have been willing to pay for the mugs. After some time had passed and they had established ownership of the mugs, test subjects wouldn't sell their mugs for less than double what they were originally willing to pay for them.[55]

The phenomenon of the winner's curse in auctions—where the auction winner is often the economic loser—is predicated on a similar principle. Once a person bids on an item, there is an element of the endowment effect in play, almost as if he or she already owns the item being auctioned. This is one of several reasons that auctions rarely prompt intelligent decisions.

Balanced Rebalancing

One way to ensure a happy medium between excessive trading and constructive optimizing is by making rebalancing more ritualized and habitual on an annual basis. Research seems to suggest that the benefits of rebalancing are virtually identical whether it is done on a quarterly, semi-annual, or annual basis,[56] but, one way or another, in some routine manner, it must be done.

Rebalancing is not a novel concept, yet it is amazing how few people sell a security or fund after it has experienced a run-up or buy more shares when their high-conviction stock pick has been beaten up. Most simply don't employ any habitual system of rebalancing. This, of course, is perfectly understandable. It is counterintuitive to sell your best positions and buy those that have been ravaged. However, that is precisely why building it into your calendar or hiring someone who will help you take care of it is of critical importance.

Besides the rebalancing of asset classes, a routine diagnostic should include a review of all fees, benchmarks, and possible redundancies within the portfolio. It should provide a robust comparison to peers, a review of managers' or advisors' adherence to their mandate(s), and an opportunity to adjust liquidity levels, scrutinize the drivers of performance, and check risk levels.

There are few things in investing that yield immediate value. This, however, is an exercise that almost always will uncover value. Our clients are often shocked to learn how much money was left on the table and how many risks were lurking right under their noses.

KEY TAKEAWAYS FROM PART III

- An investment advisor will plan for your individual needs, source and research investments to meet those needs, and monitor and rebalance your portfolio.
- If a portfolio is properly planned, the impact of the unexpected will be minimized.
- Central to good planning is the Investment Policy Statement (IPS). And central to the IPS is the asset allocation, which will be the primary driver of over 90% of returns.
- The sourcing and research process needs to be proactive rather than reactive to ensure that you are accessing best-in-class investments and have an understanding of the full opportunity set.
- Monitoring involves ongoing confirmation that those who work for you are delivering what they promised to deliver and that their work remains relevant in today's market environment.
- Rebalancing is one of the most powerful risk-mitigating tools, but few private investors do it because of behavioral biases. An objective third party can help.

PART IV

THE PRICE OF ADVICE

It is difficult to set bounds to the price unless
you first set bounds to the wish.

—Cicero

Incentives

In the late 1980s, British Petroleum, the oil and gas giant better known as BP, made a strategic decision to focus their efforts on big oil fields rather than compete for the smaller ones with countless smaller competitors. Management was also resolute about cutting costs. At the time, BP had one of the best hit rates in the oil exploration industry—hitting one new well in every five attempts, as compared to historical averages of approximately one new well in every eight attempts. Management, however, was insistent that exploration costs be cut from five dollars per barrel to one dollar. This expectation seemed completely untenable and unrealistic. It would mean BP's performance would have to go from being exceptional to being absolutely flawless. To cut 80 percent of their costs, they would have to cut all their failed attempts, forcing them to succeed on 100 percent of the holes they drilled. Explorers were up in arms.

To reinforce this idea, management announced a very simple new policy for the company: "No dry holes." Behind this policy was management's realization that their problems were not tied to poor geological skill or reckless spending but on misaligned incentives between explorers and management. If explorers struck a large reserve, they would be heroes, but if they missed, they were no worse than 80 percent of other explorers. Added to this bit of insight was the discovery that explorers were pretty good at gauging the quality of the wells they found. When they assessed the well at having a 75 percent probability of success, the wells were a hit almost every time.

When a well was given a 10 percent chance of success, it actually had about a 1 percent chance. The explorers then sold management by playing with the expected value spreadsheet. By increasing the potential payoff of a particular well, they could move a 10 percent probability hit into a category where it had a higher expected value than a 75 percent probability hit elsewhere.

Essentially, explorers became venture capitalists, speculating with BP's capital, hoping to be heroes who found the next great well. Management needed to rein the behavior in. The "no dry holes" policy forced explorers to be more focused on their decision-making processes, the quality of the underlying information, and the conviction they brought to each prospective well. The unambiguous nature of "no dry holes" forced explorers to shift their perspective from how they could make money to how they could not lose money.

The end result was not perfection. It was, however, an industry-leading 67 percent hit rate—a success story previously considered impossible.[1] The BP story serves as a fitting metaphor to the unique role of incentives and compensation structures. It demonstrates that by carefully managing incentives, investors can actually achieve a better return while taking less risk.

Regrettably, most investors seem to be in the dark when it comes to incentives. Study after study has demonstrated that investors do not have a firm understanding of the actual fees they pay, what impact fees have on returns, how fees incentivize or disincentivize performance, and what is an appropriate price for each type of opportunity. This blindness is even more dramatic when it comes to paying advisors. In fact, in one study, it was found that 73 percent of investors believed that advisors would look out for their best interests irrespective of how they were compensated.[2] Unfortunately, there is a huge collection of data suggesting that this confidence is unwarranted.

Financial blogger Josh Brown described an epiphany he had while dining at the New York Yankees Steakhouse in midtown

Manhattan. The walls in this restaurant were covered with historic baseball memorabilia, including the signed contracts of some of baseball's biggest legends. One of these contracts was the signed agreement to bring George Herman "Babe" Ruth to the Yankees from the Boston Red Sox. (This deal was believed to have doomed the Red Sox with the Curse of the Bambino, depriving them of the next eighty-six championships.) For Babe Ruth's service to the Yankees, he was promised a salary of $5,000 for the 1920 season. To further incentivize Ruth, the following clause was written into his contract:

> *The club further agrees to pay the Player and the Player agrees to accept the sum of fifty ($50) dollars for each home run made by the player during the season.*[3]

Can you guess what followed? Babe Ruth, whose first six seasons in the major league combined for a grand total of forty-nine home runs, proceeded to blast fifty-four home runs in 1920, and another fifty-nine in 1921, and averaging fifty home runs a year for the next twelve seasons.

Fifty dollars may not sound like a big deal, but this additional incentive added $2,700 to Ruth's 1920 salary, which amounted to over 50 percent of his total compensation.

What could be wrong with that? Nothing until you look at what else increased in the process. While Ruth never struck out more than fifty-eight times in his first six seasons, his strikeout totals increased to eighty in 1920 and eighty-one in 1921, and he proceeded to average about eighty strikeouts a year for the next twelve seasons. While increased strikeouts in exchange for more home runs may be acceptable in baseball, for those who are in the business of preserving capital, increasing strikeouts by almost 30 percent would be cataclysmic even if the home runs increased as well.

As these examples show, the best indication of someone's future behavior, whether in sports or investing, is found in how he or she is compensated. It is important, then, to understand the more common forms of compensation for investment advisors in order to decide which of these are more or less helpful to you in your investment decisions.

Stealth Fee Effect

Investors should look at fees not as features of investments but as the salaries or the retainers paid to the individuals charged with managing their wealth. And fees should be considered in terms of the dollars, not in terms of percentage of assets, because fees presented as a percentage of a portfolio may seem less significant than they really are. For example, a 1 percent fee may seem reasonable, but if a manager is receiving a $100,000 fee on a $10 million portfolio, it is prudent to ask whether the manager has earned this as a salary. It is a question no different from what a buyer or employer would ask about any contractor or employee. Has the manager delivered services worth $100,000 in value?

Regrettably, investors often don't give much thought to how much their advisor or asset manager is being compensated in actual dollar amounts. The brilliance of financial institutions or financial professionals being paid as a percentage of the assets they manage is what I call the *stealth fee effect*. On a monthly, quarterly, or even annual basis, investors don't see those fees taken out. They never pay an invoice and never write a check. The stealth fee structure blunts the impact of the salaries being paid out possibly to the point of neglect. Needless to say, this is great for the financial institution or professional but horrible for the investor,* and it will eventually translate into inferior or compromised returns. In

---

* This is one of the reasons we, at my firm, deliberately send an invoice every quarter. We want our clients to ask themselves how much value they are getting for their fees. And we want to keep ourselves honest by asking how we offered more value than we were paid for.

fact, studies show that in the United States nearly 25 percent of all investors' retirement savings will be eaten up by such fees as invest-ment management fees, brokerage commissions, custody expenses, and foreign exchange. In Canada, this number is actually closer to 50 percent.[4] In fact in 2009, approximately $2 billion was deducted from Canadians' mutual fund assets, as opposed to $9.5 billion clipped in the United States, which has a population that is over ten times the size of Canada.[5]

These fees are no laughing matter. There are estimates that the average mutual fund in the United States will extract nearly 4 percent of a portfolio in fees, and in Canada that number may exceed 5 per-cent.[6] What this means for investors is that their funds have to return at least 4 or 5 percent a year for them to break even much less produce a meaningful return. While very few mutual funds are actually suit-able for affluent individuals, the data is telling.

Assets Under Management

I have always struggled with the industry's infatuation with compen-sation based on assets under management (AUM). For no other ser-vice are you asked to step on the scale to ascertain the cost. Why should a $40 million investor pay $400,000 in fees when a $10 mil-lion investor pays $100,000 in fees for the same portfolio and the same amount of the advisor's time? There is also no other service where one's compensation increases in line with potential increases in risk (i.e., attempting to increase the AUM by taking greater risk). It is baffling to me that investors have accepted this reality for as long as they have. However, most institutions continue to be compensated by the size of AUM, and they continue to adopt aggressive marketing strategies to grow their AUM. These strategies may include things like promoting only the funds that were recently successful, launching new products in hot areas of the market, or adjusting part of their portfolios to mimic the benchmark. Renowned investor Charles Ellis put it succinctly when he wrote, "The profession [of investing] is about managing portfolios so as to maximize long-term returns, while the business [of investing] is about generating earnings as an investment firm."[7]

It should be clear to the investor that these two agendas—growing assets and generating superior returns—will often struggle with one another. Indeed, to the extent that an advisor can keep those two independent is the extent to which he or she will achieve real success in the profession of investing.*

There are instances where these two agendas diverge. One common example is in the use and retention of cash. Those in the business of gathering assets are generally not paid on the cash they hold. Cash, however, is one of the most robust risk-mitigating and return-enhancing tools. Anyone who sells stocks or funds of any kind will frequently reference the studies conducted by the likes of Birinyi Associates and Davis Advisors that demonstrate that if one misses the twenty, thirty, or forty best days in the market, it will drastically limit returns—suggesting that one should always stay invested in the market. The inverse scenario, however, is rather conveniently not advertised. Instead of missing the best trading days in the market, what if one missed the worst trading days in the market? The result is a much greater positive impact than one's "always-in-the-market" portfolio.[8] While no one can predict the best or worst days, this thought exercise demonstrates the value of holding cash. There are certainly occasions when markets have obviously reached a fever pitch of exuberance, and if an advisor is disincentivized to suggest the investor move to cash (i.e., fees are paid only on invested assets), it will severally impact the value of the portfolio over time.

---

* There are a growing number of funds whose only source of compensation is performance fees, with zero management fees. While generally positive, these funds must also be approached with caution to ensure the managers' interests are aligned and that they are not taking on undue risk to garner hefty incentive fees.

It is worth mentioning that fees need not be accepted at face value. Investors who are making sizeable allocations to managers or advisors who are compensated by AUM should not hesitate to negotiate their fees down. In our experience, investment managers and even advisors who are truly interested in a relationship are willing to make special accommodations. Sometimes this means getting a superior class of funds with better terms, and sometimes it simply means lowering fees.

Transaction Fees

While the stealth fee effect of AUM-based compensation may or may not concern many investors, an area that usually does is transaction fees. Transaction fees come in a variety of forms,* but the most common transaction fees are front-loaded commissions that are paid to the broker or advisor on the trade. Less common are back-loaded commissions that are paid when the asset is sold and trailing commissions that continue to be paid for as long as the asset is owned.

It is important to note that those who are compensated only on the basis of the transaction fees are often ill-equipped to offer any meaningful advice and generally less selective with whom they associate or about which deals they undertake.† As an example, I recently met with an investment manager with a portfolio of billions of dollars in real estate. I had seen many of the client's real estate investments come across my desk and wanted to take the opportunity to find out more about his company and process. We asked the manager the following question: "What might you come

---

* Pay extra notice to front-end fees and deferred-sales charges, which can be as high as 7 or 8 percent, making redemptions exceedingly difficult and costly.
† There are many exceptions to this rule. Some brokers may be brilliant experts and offer better advice than the most unconflicted advisors. However, their compensation structure does not incentivize them to do so.

across in a potential real estate property that would make you not buy it?" The manager seemed perplexed at the question. "Not buy? Why would someone not buy?" After much contemplation, the manager responded, "I guess if the property was too small." Needless to say, this is the type of answer you get from a deal junkie or broker who does not have stringent investment processes and who is compensated on the basis of transaction fees. Deal junkies, much like those selling baskets of mutual funds, are often just salespeople in disguise. They have an indiscriminate assortment of investment opportunities, targeting investors with limited sophistication and limited access to good deal flow, suggesting that it is always a good time to transact. As journalist and author Joseph Nocera once put it, "A broker with contented clients will soon be looking for another job."

Having said that, low fees should not automatically sway one's decision to the positive, as all other due diligence considerations are much more important. Many more mistakes are made on bad investment decisions than on poor fees.

Furthermore, some of the concerns around fees can be mitigated with sufficient "skin in the game" (i.e., if the investment manager has a sizeable amount of his or her net worth invested alongside yours). One of the reasons we trust pilots to bring us in for a safe landing is because any mistakes they make will impact them as much as their passengers. It should be noted, however, that unlike pilots, investment managers may be more tolerant of losses on their investments if the transaction fees they are paid exceed their personal losses. Thus, if the fees are much greater than a manager's own investment in the opportunity, then the impact of having skin in the game is muted.

Investors working with large financial institutions (even if it's just with an advisor) should be aware that there may be several other types of transaction fees that may or may not be disclosed. These include prime brokerage fees, placement agent fees, fees in connection with the provision of investment banking, foreign exchange fees, stock loan or margin fees, trading-desk activity fees, and many others.* With bonds, for example, be wary of hidden switching costs that can have a dramatic effect in a low-interest-rate environment.† This is especially painful because they are often calculated on face value, which amounts to much larger upfront fees in addition to capital gains eating away at returns.‡

In the graph is a sampling of fee types, which often come with little transparency and few explanations. These need to be well understood, probed, and considered, as they may present sharp conflicts of interests between the investor and the advisor. For example, if advisors can receive compensation from either lending or trading securities, they may choose to maximize lending income rather than portfolio value. It is therefore important to ascertain all the direct and indirect methods of compensation. It is important to know if someone's bonus is contingent upon the accumulation of assets in a very specific fund or product or just generally accumulating AUM for the firm. While I believe neither is ideal, it should be obvious why the former is much more disconcerting than the latter.

---

* It's also important to distinguish between cost and price. Just because something is not outlined as a fee does not mean that it's not part of the cost. These undisclosed fees are major blemishes on the industry.

† In general, I would be uncomfortable buying bonds out of a brokerage's inventory where the brokerage is acting as both agent and principal. This presents a whole slew of additional conflicts.

‡ Another downside to embedded transaction fees is that they are regarded as commissions. Commissions, unlike consulting fees, are not deductible as legitimate business expenses.

SAMPLING OF SUPPLEMENTAL FEES

Sales fees	Redemption fees
Trailer fees	Prime brokerage fees
Placement agent fees	Currency Conversion fees
Margin or stock Loan fees	Investment banking and M&A fees
Soft dollar fees	Embedded bond Commission fees
RRSP administration fees	Performance fees
Marketing (12b-1) fees	CEF imbedded fees
Switch fees	Account transfer fees
Liquidation fees	Inactivity fees
Referral fees	Directors' fees

With funds in particular, there are many other examples of conflicts of interest that investors should be acquainted with so they are able to ask questions, as some conflicts will not be disclosed without a nudge. One such example is found in "soft dollar arrangements," which do not need to be disclosed although they present quite a conflict to the interests of investors. An example of a soft dollar arrangement is an agreement between a particular brokerage firm and a particular money manager, whereby the money manager receives some special benefits* in exchange for marked-up brokerage commissions charged to the clients. It is thus important for an investor be educated about possible conflicts and to ask *in writing* about all possible ways that an advisor makes any money or receives any benefit.

At the time of this book's publishing, there is a movement afoot to implement Customer Relationship Model—Phase 2 (CRM2) in Canada, which will greatly increase the transparency of the aggregate fees being charged to investors. It will not, however, close up every loophole and disclose every single benefit financial professionals may

---

* These are usually cash transactions under the guise of a reimbursement for a specific expense of the money manager.

receive, and therefore both investors and their advisors must remain vigilant in the management of financial fees.

The Price of Action

Transaction fees are especially harmful because they encourage brokers and advisors to serve as knowing accomplices to one of our deep-rooted vulnerabilities: our *action bias*. The action bias is the opposite extreme of complacency, where individuals effectively ignore their portfolios. The action bias is where investors constantly trade and tinker with their portfolios, and it is among the most destructive tendencies of investors, as it makes them victims of market sentiment and all kinds of unhealthy biases.

The action bias is not limited to finance, either. Researchers from Ben-Gurion University and Hebrew University found a similar phenomenon in professional soccer. In analyzing 286 penalty kicks in championship games worldwide, they determined that given the probability distribution of where the ball may go, the optimal strategy for goalkeepers is to stay in the goal's center. However, in virtually every case, goalkeepers jumped either left or right. The goalkeepers effectively decided what they were going to do before they saw the direction of the kick. The researchers attributed this behavior to *norm theory*.[9] In other words, as it is the norm to jump, they felt compelled to do so. Further, if a goal was scored when the goalkeeper did nothing (i.e., stayed in the center), he would feel infinitely worse than if a goal was scored after he took action (i.e., jumped to one side) because it would look like he wasn't playing hard enough. Thus, although it is clear that a goalkeeper should sometimes stay put, there is significant pressure for action (i.e., the norm, the expectations of his team and the fans for him to look like he is working hard).[10] Advisors who are trying to demonstrate that they are working hard for their clients will often follow suit. It is simply more difficult to explain a poor result while sitting on the sidelines than having the same results while claiming to have tried their best.

A number of research studies seem to suggest that this bias is pervasive among private investors as well. In one particular study of institutional investors, researchers determined that, over a twenty-year period, perpetual tinkering of portfolios had cost the surveyed institutions approximately $170 billion.[11] In another study, comparing the 20 percent of investors who are most active in their portfolios with the 20 percent of investors who are least active found a discrepancy of 7.1 percent per annum. In other words, and partly due to transaction costs, those who traded the most underperformed those who traded the least by a whopping 7.1 percent per annum.[12]

Two outspoken activists in this space are University of California professors Brad Barber and Terrance Odean. Barber and Odean analyzed discount brokers in the bull market of the early to mid-1990s, where the market returned 16.4 percent, and those who traded most frequently achieved no better than 11.4 percent.[13]

Investing is not the same as trading. The more frequently your advisor transacts on your behalf, the less likely you are to be satisfied with the results. Even assuming that your advisor is honest and is not simply churning* your account, your performance will still be lower and fees will be higher than they need to be. In a worst-case scenario, churning may also be a symptom of individuals satisfying their gambling compulsion. Daniel Dorn and Paul Sengmueller investigate this impulse in *Trading as Entertainment?* The possibility that managers or advisors are sensation seekers (and not simply generating more fees) is yet another reason it behooves investors to understand what a reasonable level of activity for their portfolios is.

---

* The unethical practice of excessive trading within a client's account to generate commissions.

I've said time and again that the most important thing is focusing on the most important thing. In the case of best-practice investing, it is the goals and targets outlined in the IPS. Keeping focused on the IPS helps avoid the bias for action and any unnecessary churning of one's portfolio. Don't worry about what the markets are doing this minute, especially when they are hot or sinking like a brick. Hang tight and stick to that boring old IPS. It will pay off with buying opportunities, fewer transaction costs, and a secure financial future down the road.

Fees as a Two-Way Street

While the investor should be knowledgeable enough to not get fleeced on fees, the investor should also be knowledgeable enough to know when a good advisor is not earning enough. Fees should allow an advisor to continue doing the work you appreciate and should allow an advisor to give you the attention you need. Advisors who are making too little will be forced to take on more clients, and this can affect their focus and their performance.

There is no formula for what is sufficient for an advisor; it requires you to be thoughtful and considerate to ensure that you are getting top-tier service at a fair price. With this said, it is important to remember that bargain basement prices and highest quality counsel rarely go hand in hand. Hiring investment talent is not a commodity. If you were hiring the top corporate lawyer, the top tax accountant, or the top cardiologist, you should expect to pay top dollar for the privilege. It is no different with investing. Top talent will demand top fees.

Taking time to consider the fees of a manager or advisor means taking some time to consider your own inclinations as well. The word *humility* comes up again here. There are individuals who have decided they don't need or don't want to pay for any outside counsel. These are often a combination of know-it-alls and penny-wise, pound-foolish folks. These individuals will drive halfway across the country looking for the cheaper gas. For these poor souls, the only starting point should be the humility portion of this book.*

In general, fees should not be the primary motive for any investment decisions. While John Bogle is correct for retail investors that "the surest route to top-quartile performance is bottom-quartile expenses,"[14] for affluent investors, who can hire proper counsel, it is not quite that simple. The planning and the quality of investments is of much greater import. In fact, infinitely more money has been lost due to bad investment decisions than improper fee schedules.

Management Fees versus Advisory Fees

Fees of investment managers should be approached differently from those of brokers and advisors in part because investment managers are actually manufacturing the product and have their hands on the wheel of the asset much like property developers who take on the biggest risk but are also well compensated for it.

Investment managers who consistently earn their keep by outperforming their peers and/or their benchmarks can and should have the benefit of lucrative compensation structures. Many hedge fund managers have come to expect 20 percent of the profits as a given, and

---

* Humility is always a good start, but studies suggest that something else may be in play. Researchers from Carnegie Mellon, Stanford, and MIT found that tendencies toward being ultra-thrifty or ultra-generous with fees may be traced to the way our brains operate. When the ultra-thrifty contemplate a spending decision, they stimulate a part of the brain known as the insula, which is an area that fires up when we come in contact with a bad smell or some other unpleasant situation. The reaction can be so unpleasant that the sufferer can be put off buying entirely, even avoiding paying for the things they need. Spenders, on the other hand, activate a different part of the brain when they see something they like. For these individuals, buying decisions awaken a part of their brains called the *nucleus accumbens*, the so-called pleasure center, which starts pumping dopamine into the brain at the sight of a new shoes, a set of golf clubs, or a tempting investment opportunity, turning its victims into purchasing zombies who will readily pay without fully considering the implications.

some even more. While this may be a high price tag and despite all the criticisms of hedge fund fees, I have no problem compensating those that are best in class and whose net performance to the investor warrants it. This is no different from paying top dollar for hiring a top-tier CEO to run your company. As long as certain requirements and conditions are met that suggest a high probability of continuing to achieve good results and the opportunity to extract oneself if they do not, fees may be a red herring. The problem arises when mediocre managers who simply put up a hedge fund or private equity shingle expect such hefty fees.*

One way to mitigate the possibility of a mediocre manager is to focus on opportunities where compensation to management is back-loaded. This is where the economics become advantageous for the operator or investment manager *only after* the investors have been properly compensated for the investment and perhaps even seen a return of their capital. This would include having a hurdle or preferred returns for the investors. High-water marks† are also essential components for funds with public market investments. Besides assuring that they are included as part of the term sheet, investors should verify that the fund has a perpetual high-water mark without any resets (which would defeat the entire purpose of a high-water mark).

---

* It should be noted that fees are entirely unregulated. It is entirely up to the discernment of the buyer to decide whether or not to transact with someone who charges outlandish fees.

† A high-water mark is the peak of net asset value when the funds were provided to the manager. This number is important because most hedge funds collect both a management fee and a performance fee, which is a percentage of the profits. It is important that the performance fee (i.e., profits) be assessed as true gains to the funds, not gains that came after losses. For example, if an investor invests $250,000 in 2008 and that investment's value falls to $150,000, and in 2009, the hedge fund produces 100 percent returns so that the investment is now worth $300,000, this individual should have to pay performance fees only on the $50,000 gained, not on the full $150,000, of which $100,000 was the investor's principal.

Investors must develop a level of sophistication where fees are warranted for each type of investment. For example, where does a 1 percent management fee make sense? Where does a 2 percent management fee make sense? Where does an additional 20 percent incentive fee (i.e., 20 percent of the profits) make sense? Investors are constantly making poor buying decisions with regard to fees. For example, in today's low-interest-rate environment, there are people paying for guaranteed flat or negative performance.[15] Some Canadian money market funds are charging a trailer of twenty-five basis points for funds with zero returns. Why would anyone in his or her right mind do that? What is the manager doing to earn those twenty-five basis points? Why don't you just put it in the bank and give them the pleasure of paying you the same twenty-five basis points instead?

The investor or the investor's advisor must always look at compensation in relation to both the performance of the opportunity on a net basis and the market rate for these investments. If the manager is not consistently outperforming his or her benchmark, after all fees have been built in, other options should be explored.

Avoid Paying Retail

The one thing that affluent investors must absolutely avoid doing is buying retail. In most cases, they should be able to buy at wholesale prices or go into limited partnerships or aggregate with other investors to meet the high minimums of best-in-class managers. I recently heard from a hedge fund manager that some of our clients are invested in and who has a proven track record of consistent outperformance. The manager informed us that they had developed a retail offering of their strategy. Because the liquidity terms were better, we wanted to see if it would be appropriate for our clients. We asked the investor relations person at the fund what the difference was between the retail product and the limited partnership besides the liquidity.* She replied with three words: "Fees, fees, and fees." For starters, there is 1.5 percent commission to the broker, an additional 1.0 percent commission to the issuing bank, another 1.0 percent commission to the advisor plus a twenty-five-basis-point trailer, and an additional 1.25 percent fee to the manager. When it was all said and done, there were 9 percent in fees in the first year before the investor made a dime. On a $300,000 investment, that would translate $27,000 out of the investor's pocket before a single investment decision is made. Naturally, we decided our clients should stick to the limited partnership. All the fees at the various layers of the retail distribution chain have ruined the prospects of what was otherwise an exceptional investment opportunity.

Final Word on Compensation for Advisors

It is my firm belief that the absolute ideal compensation structure with an advisor should be commensurate with the value they offer. In an ideal world, it should be on the basis of outcome. If financial advisors are truly trusted advisors who can serve a family, irrespective of where the funds reside or where they are invested, the only way to do that is to compensate them well for the time they spend and the value they bring to the family. That is why more often than not a family's trusted advisor and mentor will be an accountant or perhaps even a lawyer. An accountant does not take a percentage of savings that he or she has provided to a client, in the same way a doctor who saves a life does not take a percentage of a patient's future earnings. Accountants, doctors, lawyers, and just about every other trusted professional does

---

* Incidentally, the very first open-ended fund, which is the structure of today's mutual funds, was created in March 1924 by Edward G. Leffler to provide liquidity. This has allowed an untold number of investors access to pooled investment vehicles. Though with all the criticism of the mutual fund industry today, the question is, at what price?

not benefit from the upside or the downside. They stand alongside the clients and hold the clients' hands through thick and thin. Financial advisors should not be any different. Their clients should see on an ongoing basis the value they offer, and they should build a relationship that is meaningful, long-lasting, and transformational, not short-lived and transactional. In the absence of this arrangement, at least ensure that all the best practices in this book are adhered to.

Alignment with Investment Managers

In addition to fees, investors should be concerned that the structure of ownership aligns with their interests. For example, they should be attuned to how much of the investment manager's net worth is invested alongside their clients. Unlike advisors, who are paid for advice, investment managers are paid for performance and should therefore share in both the upside and downside consequences of their decisions. Since you cannot (yet) penalize poor performance, the best way to ensure alignment is to ensure that investment managers are eating their own cooking. This is most commonly achieved by confirming (ideally in writing) that a large portion of the manager's net worth is invested alongside your capital.

Misalignment is so significant that it could have cataclysmic effects, not just for the company but also for the industry or the economy as a whole. Over the last several decades in the United States, fixed-rate stock options made the corporate culture quite toxic. By providing someone with only upside and without sharing the downside risk, these options incentivized a generation of management to take ever greater risks for self-gain. For example, managers are often incentivized to increase a stock repurchase in order to raise the share price even if the company's shares are demonstrably overvalued. Being diligent and limiting these kinds of conflicts is not just in our own best interests but also in the interests of society as a whole.

KEY TAKEAWAYS FROM PART IV

- Advisory and asset management fees are fundamentally different because asset managers are closer to risk.
- For any fees, there has to be an honest assessment about whether the value provided is equal to the dollars spent.
- Virtually any fee structure has pros and cons, but some cons are diametrically opposed to the interests of investors. This is a problem, especially when the full range of fees are not properly disclosed.
- Besides the level of performance, it is also important to understand what kind of fees are warranted for what kind of investments.
- Ultra-high net worth investors can often avoid paying retail by receiving or negotiating better prices and terms. Always ensure you are not passing on the opportunity to do so.

THE MEASURES
OF SUCCESS

*If a rich man is proud of his wealth, he should not be praised
until it is known how he employs it.*

—Socrates

I f you properly executed everything we have discussed thus far over an investment horizon, it should translate into positive risk-adjusted results. After all, aren't positive results what investing is all about? However, results and performance are not as simply determined as one would think. Past performance seems to be the only objective measure of someone's abilities, but past performance is not indicative of future performance. In fact, it may be an indicator of an imminent reversal. Countless studies have shown that funds that have outperformed their peers for several years will likely not outperform them going forward. A large run-up could mean the asset or portfolio is overpriced with a high probability of decline down the road. This, coupled with the facts that three-quarters of all active managers will underperform the S&P 500[1] and that the annual return on actively managed funds will lag behind the Wilshire 5000 Stock Index,[2] should encourage us to approach past track records with caution.

Track Record

Imagine that somebody walks into a boardroom, throws a pitch deck in front of you, and tells you that they've developed or employed a unique trading strategy that has translated into six straight years of exceptional outperformance. The management team is made up of brilliant people—PhDs, CFAs, actuaries, and Harvard MBAs. Moreover, the team's strategy made sense to you, your due diligence on the operation came back clean with its six-year track record verified, you knew other people who have invested in the fund, and all the references testified to the immaculate integrity of the people involved. At this point, you need to ask yourself if the fund manager has a sufficiently long track record for you to consider investing in the fund.

Hold that thought. Let us delve into a bit of data and then return to the question. Eugene Fama's pioneering research of the 1960s confirmed that the top-performing funds in one year were not more likely to outperform their peers the following years.[3] Some research even suggested that top-performing quartile managers in one quarter were actually more likely to end up in bottom quartiles the next quarter.[4] This was an amazing discovery in the middle of the twentieth century, but it is even more remarkable that today, fifty years later, this continues to be a discovery to most investors.

Now, keeping in mind this research, imagine that, for the sake of a fun experiment, we put 10,000 equally (and objectively) mediocre* investment managers into a room. Theoretically, we would expect each of them to have a fifty-fifty chance of either outperforming or underperforming the market. In other words, this year 5,000 of these 10,000 managers will outperform market, and 5,000 will underperform the market. Next year, the team of 5,000 successful managers will be narrowed down to 2,500 outperformers and 2,500 underperformers. The following year, 1,250, then just over 625, then just over 310, and after six years the group of outperformers will be down to 155. By this point, there will be many other indicators of success. These 155 managers will receive extensive media coverage, and capital will come flooding in. They will attract some of the brightest young graduates from Wharton, Harvard, and every other Ivy League program. Novice investors will start mimicking every move they make, and eventually even these managers will start believing that they have discovered the

---

* *Mediocre* being defined by being not one iota better than the top 50 percent of investment managers and not worse than the bottom 50 percent of investment managers.

magic sauce, perhaps publishing a book or two on their recipe for success. Now imagine that one or two of these managers walked into your office and presented you with the opportunity to invest in their funds. The only difference between the managers who presented at the start of this section and these 155 managers is that now you have full knowledge of the experiment. How would you feel about investing with our 155 stars?

Most people would be tempted to consider an allocation with the first set of managers. Seeing the opportunity, they would jump into the fund, envisioning each manager as the young Warren Buffett of our time. However, most people would be cautious of jumping in with the second set of managers because they know that the experiment is continuing and there is a significant probability that they will underperform in year seven and an even higher likelihood of underperforming by year eight. In other words, each day is a new day in the market, and outperformance in any given year does not offer a golden ticket to outperformance in the next. To dramatize this point, forget human money managers and just use monkeys, as Burton Malkiel did in his 1973 best seller, *A Random Walk Down Wall Street*. In his book, he experimented with one hundred monkeys randomly throwing darts at a newspaper's financial pages and found that this method constructed portfolios that performed as well as those created by experts in the field.

Given that there are considerably more than 10,000 advisors, money managers, mutual fund managers, or hedge fund managers in North America alone,* this experiment tends to play itself out more often than we realize, and it favors those who got lucky early. For the investors, this is referred to *sequence-of-returns risk*. For investment

---

* Estimates have pegged just the number of mutual funds and various hedge funds in North America to be closer to 40,000. This does not include brokers and financial advisors, many of whom are also constructing portfolios of individual securities whose numbers are estimated to be between 350,000 and 450,000.

managers, some have referred to this as the *Matthew effect*.* The basic premise is that those who get lucky early derive way more benefit from their good fortune. For example, investment managers who were lucky in the first five years of their careers will be touted as young superstars, receive media acclaim, and have money flowing in, which will allow them to hire people who may help them keep the ship steady going forward (if their egos do not get in the way).† Those who got lucky in the next five years, however, will have a very difficult time getting the full benefit of that good fortune because by that point, people will have seen years of mediocre performance, and any positive performance will be largely accredited to luck—unlike the former scenario, where positive performance would be largely attributed to skill. (This research has been shown in other areas as well. It has been found that those who are hot early in their careers are less likely to shield themselves from major losses down the road.[5]) The bottom line is some managers get lucky by *when* they get lucky.

This law of averages is not uncommon outside of investing. Historically, the worst teams in baseball have beaten the best teams in a series 15 percent of the time.[6] A few well-timed home runs, one or two errors, and you're there. Likewise, for individual players, there is no information that can be gathered from three, five, or even ten consecutive at-bats. Any five at-bats will not in any way influence a player's contract negotiations at the end of the season. Over the course of 162-game season, however, the best teams in baseball rise to

---

* The notion that the rich get richer and the poor get poorer.
† Sowood Capital Management was a recent example of this phenomenon. The hedge fund was led by a group of all-stars who left the Harvard Management Company to start their own fund in 2004. The highly celebrated group was quickly showered with more capital than most managers expect to have in a lifetime, including $500 million from Harvard itself. In short order, they were managing over $3 billion. However, thanks to greed, excessive leverage, and a host of qualitative challenges, the fund spiraled downward and would have blown up if not for Citadel's last-minute salvaging of the last $1.4 billion of the portfolio.

the top, and after seeing five hundred at-bats, you can get a pretty good sense of which players have exceptional skill.

So, what is the equivalent of 162 games in investing? What is considered a long enough track record? As always, the answer depends on the strategy. All else being equal, investment managers who employ a high-frequency trading strategy may only need a few years of consistency to demonstrate their trading abilities.* Those who rarely trade and instead employ a deep value strategy or invest in distressed real estate may need ten years of history to demonstrate themselves, and an infrastructure or land development manager may need decades to demonstrate best-in-class performance.

The reality is that it is almost impossible to determine on the basis of past performance alone whether or not the returns will be sustained, what risks lurk around the corner, or how much luck was involved. Thus there is a need to understand risk exposures, the size of the fund relative to the opportunity set, and which market conditions may be lethal toward any particular strategy. Without that broader context, if looking at past performance alone, statisticians estimate that it would take at least forty years to definitively conclude that the returns from a specific portfolio are attributable to skill rather than to chance.[7] Even then, it's a best guess, and anything is possible in year forty-one.

Predictive Process

Professor Michael Wheeler at the Harvard Business School asserted that "even Niccolò Machiavelli, the cataloger of each and every lever that a prince can pull in the pursuit of power, acknowledged that 'I believe that it is probably true that fortune is the arbiter of half the

---

* Notably, trading ability alone is not necessarily a predictor of success. Other considerations, including leverage or exposure, extreme macroeconomic environments, and higher levels of assets under management can all contribute to the success or failure of a strategy.

things we do, leaving the other half to be controlled by ourselves.'"[8] History may teach and inform us, but it cannot predict for us. Someone may have been a successful real estate operator for twenty years and then made a horrific mistake by taking on an irresponsible amount of debt. Someone else might have been a trusted broker and then developed a gambling problem in his later years. It is fairly intuitive to us that any deviation is possible, but research suggests that deviation is actually probable. That is why we constantly revert back to the fact that investment decisions should be much more about the process and fundamentals than about outcomes and performance. The challenge is that outcomes are objective and a good process appears subjective. In addition, one can make a poor decision and still prosper or make a proper decision and falter. Notwithstanding these two challenges, for investors and advisors, the focus should not be on short-term outcomes but on process, which is the only reliable safeguard one can employ.

Take for example, Robert Zuccaro's Grand Prix Fund. In 1998, the fund had astonishing performance of 112 percent. As if that wasn't good enough, in 1999 the fund returned 148 percent. As 2000 got under way, the fund was already up over 30 percent. Investors took note, and nearly $400 million was piled into the fund.[9] Who would have guessed that by the end of 2000, the Grand Prix Fund would be down 33 percent? Down by 56 percent in 2001? Down by 47 percent in 2002?[10] Within a few years, the fund officially blew up. Looking back, you have to ask whether Zuccaro's earlier performance was simply good luck. Or was his later performance simply bad luck? And to what extent did his investing acumen—or, conversely, his ineptitude—play a role? Digging into the history, it turns out that as Zuccaro's fund was sinking, he was assuring investors that the volatility was to be expected and, to really get the benefit of his strategy, one had to buy and hold the fund for years. However, when a reporter from

Forbes looked at his churn rate,* he found a portfolio turnover of 717 percent, a number that in no way resembled buy-and-hold value creation.[11] There was an obvious disconnect between the strategy employed and the stated mandate. It was a classic mistake, and spotting this simple flaw in the process could have left a group of people nearly $400 million richer.

Our brains are wired with an *outcome bias*, meaning that we tend to judge our decisions based on the outcome rather than whether we made the right decision at the time. For example, if I convince my workaholic friend to take a night off and go to a restaurant for his birthday and then we both get food poisoning, he may blame me for the illness when the decision was correct at the time and the outcome could never have been foretold. In his mind, the decision was a bad one based on the outcome. The fact is that the ability to clearly see cause and effect is a fantastically complex one. Neuroscientist Michael Gazzaniga found that humans will readily interpret cause and effect without sufficient information to do so. The left hemisphere of the brain houses what Gazzaniga has called "the interpreter," which uses inputs from everything around us to explain our world. The interpreter works without considering probabilities, randomness, or the completeness of information. In one study, a split-brain patient (a patient who has had the corpus callosum severed, leaving no communication between the left and right hemispheres of the brain) was shown a picture in each visual field and asked to point to one of four other pictures that it would relate to. The researchers then asked the left hemisphere—the only hemisphere that can talk— why the left hand had chosen its related picture. This was effectively

---

* *Churning* generally refers to the unethical practice of brokers excessively trading to generate commissions for themselves at the expense (not the interest) of the client. Here it refers to the rate at which the portfolio was turned over by buying and selling securities. A high churn rate is indicative of an aggressive trading strategy; it also results in high transaction fees and could generate a significant tax liability. Value-oriented managers do not have high churn rates.

asking the left brain to explain why he was pointing to a picture it had never seen (as the decision to point with the left hand had been made by the right brain). The patient should have responded, "I don't know." Instead, without a moment's hesitation, the patient came up with a sensible story. Further studies confirmed that we are wired to interpret—look at outcomes and instantaneously come up with reasons for those outcomes—irrespective of the facts.[12]

For better or worse, humans are wired to make cause-and-effect judgments. To dramatize this point, in the early 1990s, David Leinweber found that butter production in Bangladesh was the single best predictor of the S&P 500 performance,[13] and this sent an army of Wall Street traders on the hunt for insights into Bangladeshi butter industry. While this story is amusing, it also highlights the challenges for investors who can easily make poor investment decisions on the basis of misguided assessments about cause and effect.

Knowing about our tendency to tell ourselves stories and sway toward an outcome bias will not remove the bias, but it will help us distinguish between positive performance with poor fundamentals and positive performance with strong fundamentals. For example, in blackjack if the cards come up on an eighteen and the player adds another card to get a three to win, the player may have had a wonderful result, but it was a poorly calculated decision. Investors (and especially advisors) must develop the ability to distinguish between the quality of a decision and the outcome of that decision. This means returning to the fundamentals and understanding why a particular manager or investment opportunity has a high probability of success. With all these cautions, it should be noted that past performance may still be a useful screen for determining which opportunities are worthy of further analysis. Those who have demonstrated consistently poor performance are unlikely to change. Likewise, if one posts consistently positive results, despite the limitations of tracking past performance, it is certainly indicative that the manager was either very smart or very lucky, and neither type is terrible company to keep.

With few exceptions, it is highly unlikely that an investor will be able to see a forty-year track record from any manager. Thus, in making any investment decision, we have to rely on what we have seen in the past to make estimations about the future. But the question must be asked: Besides understanding the fundamentals and ensuring that a manager has all the necessary qualities, is there any way of using performance to better determine the skill of the manager? The answer may lie in an aphorism widely attributed to Mark Twain: "History doesn't repeat itself but it often rhymes."[14]

In practice, for most institutional investors, a three- to five-year rolling average may be a sufficient indicator to demonstrate persistence of performance. Though even here, it is important to note our tendency to have a *recency bias* where we overweight predictions about the future based on what happened recently. In the process, we may discount the long-standing historical performance of a particular manager for a recent aberration.[15] If you are going to use past performance as an indicator of any kind, be careful not to discount nonrecent performance. It is no less important.

Wading through all these biases and confusions, what we are left with is the paradox of performance. Performance is the ultimate goal of our investment pursuits, yet it may be among the weaker indicators of future success. On the one hand, performance measures need to be timely to be relevant for decisions about hiring, retaining, or replacing investment managers. On the other hand, it takes many years before it is possible to determine whether the results were obtained by skill or by luck. The shorter the performance evaluation period, the greater the chances of sampling error, and the less of an indication it is of future performance. As Charles Ellis noted, "By the time performance statistics are good enough to act on, the time for action is long past."[16]

Performance may be a decent screen, but is not a sufficient data point in making any investment decisions. What seems more relevant is the ability to distinguish between skill and luck in investing and past performance. This will be the subject of the section ahead.

LUCK AND STREAKS

How do you know if luck was involved? Michael Mauboussin suggested that the litmus test of luck's involvement in any endeavor is whether you can lose on purpose.[17] In chess, for example, you can easily maneuver yourself into defeat. However, if you play roulette or any slot machine, it is impossible to lose on purpose. Investing works in a similar way. Theoretically, one could choose investments where you could almost certainly lose and yet miraculously turn a profit. Conversely, you can have a bulletproof strategy and still lose your shirt. Luck is certainly ever present and must be acknowledged by any investor.

The greater the role of luck the greater the variability of results. This is evident when comparing the legends of checkers or chess with the stars of blackjack or poker. Mathematician Marion Tinsley was the greatest checker player who ever lived. The man never lost a world championship match, and in his forty-five-year career he lost only seven games. Two of those losses were to a computer program. This record is a manifestation of a large amount of skill and a small amount of luck. In blackjack, where luck has a much greater role in the outcome, there has never been a multiyear winner in the World Series of Blackjack.

We would like to believe that investing is more akin to chess and checkers than it is to blackjack or poker, but history has proven otherwise. And that inherent uncertainty is what investors get paid for. Rather than trying to avoid this uncertainty, investing requires a healthy balance between the extremes of relying on blind luck and believing that any amount of tools or theories will deliver certainty. Everyone wants to mitigate their downside and avoid painful outcomes, but while it is possible to hedge out many risks and uncertainties, it is impossible to protect against every possible scenario. Therefore even conservative investing is more like poker than checkers, as poker and investing require both luck and skill.[18]

My partners and I frequently joke that if we had to select managers and forced to choose between someone who is very smart and someone who is very lucky, we'd go with lucky any day of the week. The reality, of course, is that luck is never sufficient, but it also cannot be ignored. Perhaps the ideal approach was the balanced view of former US president Thomas Jefferson when he said, "I'm a great believer in luck, and I find the harder I work the more I have of it." When hard work and every best practice is properly applied to investing, it is quite amazing how lucky we can get.

Streaks

There are many degrees of luck. There is obviously some degree of luck involved in flawlessly executing any intelligently laid plan – i.e. where skill is dominant and luck is secondary. Then there is the more dramatic luck of winning the lottery – i.e. where luck is dominant and skill is secondary (or nonexistent). Somewhere in the middle is the phenomenon of streaks. Stephen Jay Gould, the noted scientific historian and prolific writer, once commented that "long streaks are, and must be, a matter of extraordinary luck imposed on great skill." Gould was responding to Joe DiMaggio's historic fifty-six-game hitting streak, a record that he set in 1941 and that stands to this very day. In the years that followed, many critics claimed that DiMaggio was just extremely lucky. Gould conceded that some luck was likely involved, but he qualified it by saying that it could not have happened without a great deal of skill.

There have been many other notable examples of lucky streaks in sports. Wayne Gretzky, who is one of the most accomplished hockey players to ever take the ice, maintains the record for most consecutive games with a point scored. In basketball, Hall of Famer Wilt Chamberlin holds the record for consecutive made field goals. Chamberlin's career field goal percentage of 54 percent, places him among the best in the league's history. Returning to baseball, only forty-two players have had hitting streaks of thirty games or more. If you were to average out the lifetime batting average of these players (.311) that would put this group among the top one hundred players in the history of baseball.[19] The bottom line is that whenever streaks surface, they tend to be associated with a fairly high degree of skill.

Gould articulated a commonly shared belief in the scientific community that neither luck nor skill alone is enough to maintain extraordinarily long streaks where variability of results is high. The same seems to hold true for investing. Andrew Mauboussin and Sam Arbesman have spent four decades analyzing mutual fund performance and the streaks therein. After capturing data on over fifty thousand mutual fund years and over ten thousand mutual funds around the world, they discovered that the funds that had any extraordinary streaks also had significantly higher average performance and outperformed their benchmarks much more often than the average fund.[20] This correlation between the funds' streaks and the funds' outperformance seems to again suggest that extraordinary streaks emerge from a combination of both luck and skill.

If streaks are, in fact, indicative of a manager possessing this wonderful confluence of both luck and skill, it would seem important to identify streaks. I believe that there are three questions one could ask to help in identifying prevailing streaks of success.

1. How do I know it's a streak?

First and foremost, consider how far away from baseline performance the manager or the fund is. Amos Tversky and Daniel Kahneman have written about a bias they like to call *belief in the law of small numbers*,[21] suggesting that humans are regularly wrong on their intuitions of appropriate sample sizes. For example, five at-bats in the context of baseball may be virtually insignificant, so if someone gets a base hit five times in a row, that should not be deemed a streak. It is important to consider how long is long enough for an anomaly to be considered a streak in whatever domain you are looking into. Determine what the historic averages are and how far a manager's performance has deviated from them.

2. How much accounts for luck and how much accounts for skill?

Consider to what extent skill and to what extent luck might have contributed to a streak. It is unlikely that this questions could be answered in any scientific way, but merely analyzing how many things could have gone wrong and what the expected outcomes might have been will provide some insight. This question also requires a qualitative evaluation of the manager, including a look at processes and philosophies and how fittingly performance has matched those processes and philosophies. For example, was positive performance largely driven by one security that had astronomical growth, while all others appeared to be fruitless? Or were the majority of securities performing positively, as the manager believed they would?

3. What is the likelihood of continuing on this trajectory?

One must approach streaks with extreme caution, but this is easier said than done. Streaks, especially long streaks, inspire within us an *illusion of safety*. In a study of mice,* researchers found that they could be conditioned for safety, which meant that where there was a repeated absence of danger, the mice would become bolder and take

---

* Researchers took mice that had previously been conditioned to get an electric shock whenever they entered a particular room and conditioned them to a unique series of sounds that indicated no shocks would be administered. After about ten repetitions of these sounds, the mice came to associate them with the absence of danger. Feeling that they were safe, the mice were considerably more daring than any mice were before being conditioned for safety.

on considerably more risk.[22] This illusion of safety has found victims outside the animal kingdom with even the savviest economists. In 1921, the Dow Jones Industrial Average began at 71.995. It peaked at 381.17 on September 3, 1929, for an increase of 430 percent. At this point, one of the most highly regarded economists in US history, Irving Fisher, announced that the markets had reached "a permanently high plateau." Within just a few weeks came the crash of 1929 and the Great Depression that followed. In 1932, with the Depression still in full swing, the Dow reached a low point of 41.22 and didn't return to 300 until 1954.[23]

There are countless stories of economists making poor forecasts, but investors are equally susceptible to making similar assessments about their money managers. The *illusion of safety* often prompts individuals to invest more and more money with those that are having a winning streak even when taking money off the table may be a more prudent decision.

Closing Thoughts on Luck

Our discussion of luck highlights the need to temper our excitement over both impressive and unimpressive recent performance numbers. Smart investors will sometimes lose and foolish ones will sometimes win. By definition, luck is involved wherever the outcome is unpredictable. This is true whether an investor is trying to ride a lucky streak or to cash in on the inevitable reversal of fortunes.

Earlier in this book we referenced a phenomenon called the *gambler's fallacy*, which is the belief that if a particular behavior is repeatedly observed, then in next sequence of these behaviors the opposite results are more likely. Thus if a flipped coin lands on heads ten times in a row, the gambler's fallacy is that there is a high probability of the coin landing on tails in the next ten tosses. The reality is that every coin toss has an equal chance of landing on either side, and previous tosses do not impact the toss results of the future. In investing, one needs to be aware that many consecutive positive streaks don't necessarily mean the next year will be a slump in the same way that poor performers of yester-year are more likely to outperform all their peers in the future. Regardless, our understanding of luck will likely shape our invest-ment philosophy, as it has for countless eminent investors in the past.

Investment legends George Soros and Warren Buffett, for exam-ple, present an ideal illustration of the role of luck in investing and their different approaches to it. There most obvious difference between their investment philosophies is that Soros will look at an item and buy it for a dollar when his analysis suggests this item will be worth two dollars in the foreseeable future. Buffett, on the other hand, buys that same item for a dollar only when his analysis suggests that the item is worth two dollars today and it is unlikely to cost less than a dollar anytime in the future. Both are legitimate strategies, but they differ in how heavily they weigh luck. Soros's strategy is deeply thoughtful and well researched, but it relies on the accuracy of his pre-dictions about an ever-changing future. In the absence of prophesy, this involves some measure of luck. Buffett's strategy, on the other hand, relies on the exactness of the bargains he found today, and not the realization of specific events in the future. It is because of Soros's heavier dependence on luck that you will find far fewer global macro* investors (Soros followers) than value† investors (Buffett followers) with decades of success and who are still around to tell the story.

Even individuals whose orientation is macroeconomic tend to adopt a respectful attitude toward value investing. The most notable example of this was, in fact, the father of macroeconomics, John Maynard

---

* Generally, global macro strategies involve trading based on analysis about the macroeconomic conditions and developments of the world. Investors in these strate-gies are often reliant on forecasts about political shifts, interest rate movements, gov-ernment policies, and other universal systemic factors, all of which dictate the investor's movements in and out of markets with the shift in trends.

† Simply put, this strategy involves buying financial assets for less than their intrinsic value, determined through fundamental analysis, and placing far less regard for the value placed on the asset by markets.

Keynes. In 1921, after assuming his role as the head of King College's investments at the University of Cambridge, Keynes convinced the college to carve out a portion of the funds for a more speculative strategy. This would allow Keynes to use his skills as an economist to forecast the markets and make investments accordingly. Regrettably, this proved to be disastrous, with the portfolio under Keynes's management lagging the UK equity markets by double digits. To make matter worse, Keynes did not anticipate the crash of 1929. This proved to be a wake-up call for him. From then on, Keynes, one of the most venerated economists in history,* ceased being a forecaster or a market timer and shifted his focus to value investing. He looked at undervalued stocks and distressed companies that nonetheless had healthy cash flows and paid generous dividends. This pivot proved correct, as Keynes continued to manage the fund until his death in 1946. Throughout his tenure, the funds compounded at an annual rate of 9.1 percent while the UK equity market fell at an average rate of nearly 1 percent per annum over the same period.[24]

Keynes began his career, like most of us, overly enthusiastic about the stock market. And we have good reason to be enthusiastic, as markets have skyrocketed over time. Just think that the S&P 500 closed at 44.06 on its opening day in March 4, 1957. By 2016, it was hovering around the 2100s—over forty-seven times its value at inception. The growth of capital markets has been explosive. In 1990, the value of all publicly traded stocks totaled $19 trillion. By 2000, that number reached $31 trillion, and over the next ten years—a period often called "the lost decade"—publicly traded stocks rose to over $54 trillion.[25] And the trajectory will likely continue. Unfortunately, enthusiasm over legitimate long-term growth spills into enthusiasm during inflated and exuberant parts of the cycle. Riding this enthusiasm is simply relying on luck, as prices rise to astronomical levels, before they inevitably crash down to earth and the luck runs out.

---

* *The Economist* labeled him "Britain's most famous 20th-century economist."

Value investing takes not only more training and knowledge, but it is extremely difficult for most individuals to do because it requires making counterintuitive decisions all the time (i.e., selling your best performers and buying more of your underperformers). It also rarely gives the immediate payoff of a well-timed piece of luck, but it is the very reason why Buffett, Graham, Lynch, and Klarman have maintained their reign for decades while many speculators and forecasters have come and gone.

BENCHMARKS

Benchmarks mean different things to different people, but for affluent investors, the primary role of benchmarks should be quite specific. Recall that the driving force of the entire investment process is the IPS. In the IPS, there are selected asset classes whose purpose is to collectively achieve a specific return for the entire portfolio over an investment horizon. That required return has been generated through a realistic assessment of the individual's financial needs and aspirations. That number is the investor's most important benchmark. It is static and does not get adjusted in bull markets or bear markets unless there is a change in the needs, aspirations, or personal circumstances of the investor.

In contrast to investors, when investment managers reference benchmarks, they are usually referring to common indices like the S&P 500, the Wilshire 5000, the Russell 3000, or the MSCI World Index. These can certainly be helpful in comparing or assessing funds, but for advisor to assess the success of their clients by comparing them to these indices is problematic. For one, unlike private investors, the index neither contains nor requires any cash. The index has no life expectancy requirements and does not have to compensate for distributions to meet living requirements. The index does not require a rate of return that keeps up with inflation or concern itself with capital preservation. Along the same lines, the index pays no taxes, has no transaction costs, nor any of the fees associated with managing its assets. Finally, the index bears equal risk on the way up as it does on the way down. This may be wonderful in good times but is usually inadequate in times of turmoil. Lastly, while the various indices exist indefinitely, portfolios generally have a time frame. Whether one is looking to transfer wealth to children, prepare for retirement, or achieve any other aspiration, there is a time line that investors (and their advisors) must consider, and risk must be managed accordingly. All these reasons and constraints are unique to each investor, and thus the index is a poor benchmark for any investor's overall portfolio.

Indices, however, cannot be completely discounted. In fact, they are exceptionally helpful and perhaps even necessary for benchmarking the underlying asset classes in a portfolio, ensuring that they are behaving as they should be behaving. To properly benchmark, a healthy basis of comparison with the outside world is needed. Every advisor should employ both a relative return benchmark for each of the asset classes, which is dynamic, and an absolute return benchmark for the overall portfolio, which is static. For example, perhaps a particular investor needs at least a 7.2 percent return over an investment horizon to meet all of his or her personal needs and objectives. This will be the static portfolio benchmark. To achieve this benchmark will require the following asset allocations:

Asset Class	Target Allocation	Expected Return	Attribution
Real Assets	25%	10%	2.5%
Equities	15%	7%	1.1%
Uncorrelated*	15%	8%	1.2%
Credit	10%	9%	0.9%
Private Equity	5%	12%	0.6%
Fixed Income	20%	4%	0.8%
Cash	10%	1%	0.1%
RETURN			**7.2%**

---

* *Uncorrelated* refers to investment strategies that employ either hedging and/or trading, which produces results that are not correlated with equities or any other asset class.

Assuming that the expected returns are determined intelligently and conservatively, these will become the static benchmarks of the asset classes.

To make sure that the upward or downward fluctuations make sense, the dynamic benchmarks will also need to be referenced to illustrate how the various investments have performed relative to their respective peer groups. This can be achieved by identifying the most fitting comparison to each asset class. For example, the Russell 3000 may be a useful comparison for US public equities, the MSCI REIT for real estate, Barclays Aggregate Bond Index for bonds, three-month T-bill for cash, and any of the HFRI* indices for a variety of uncorrelated strategies. There are numerous indices in the market, allowing one to easily identify a dynamic benchmark for almost any asset class or investment strategy.

Properly benchmarking the performance of asset managers or fund managers within each of those asset classes is another consideration that requires analysis. While it may be somewhat difficult emotionally, it is the least complicated measure of success. It is answering the simple question of whether the manager is doing what was promised. Effectively, the job of the investor is not measuring investment managers' *performance* but measuring their *conformance*—in other words, to what extent the managers conformed to their stated objective from the point of view of strategy, market response, risk undertaken, accuracy of thesis, and returns under various market conditions. As an added precaution, it helps to compare managers against their peers who are executing similar strategies in the same asset class.

Focusing on conformance also means investigating all sharp aberrations, whether they are positive or negative, as a manager that drastically exceeded their peers may have taken more risk than their peers. Even though rarely will anyone complain about outlandishly

---

* This refers to the 150-plus indices on various hedge fund strategies, provided by Hedge Fund Research, Inc. for benchmarking and performance measurement purposes.

positive performance, few affluent investors want to find themselves on the opposite extreme when the pendulum swings back. For this very reason, conformance is a useful tool. And it's equally useful for advisors as it is for money managers, notwithstanding that the metrics may be different. Advisors need to be measured on the extent to which they did what they told you they would do, the extent to which they protected you from yourself, and the extent to which you have peace of mind. There are many criteria to measure the performance of advisors, but these three should not be negotiable.

Benchmark Cautions

There are many potential issues with using benchmarks that investors need to be aware of. One of the oldest tricks in an underperforming manager's book is comparing the client's portfolio with the wrong benchmark, perhaps even the wrong time period or in the wrong currency. In a similar vein, neither investors nor advisors should oscillate between different benchmarks. Stick to the one that best mirrors the type of assets involved, write it into the IPS, and do not shift again unless there is a compelling reason to do so.

An issue that is common among even the largest financial institutions is comparing an entire portfolio to an index instead of comparing the respective asset class to specific indices. Comparing a portfolio of futures, REITs, principal protected notes, or hedge funds to the S&P 500 is a useless exercise. It does not tell us anything about the specific investments. Take, for example, a hypothetical technology fund called XYZ that returned 38 percent in 2003. That might have been exceptional by most standards and have been outperforming the S&P 500 by nearly 10 percent that year. However, when compared to the Goldman Sachs Technology Index, which returned more than 50 percent in 2003, XYZ appears to be an underperformer.

The sizes of holdings are another important consideration when choosing a benchmark. The problem with benchmarking the majority of active managers against the S&P 500 is that it may be comparing apples and oranges. Research suggests that most active managers' portfolios consist of stocks with much smaller market capitalizations than the S&P 500. This may conceal the skill or the ineptitude of the manager. If the average market cap of the holdings is closer to mid- or small-cap stocks, those will often triumph in the decade where large cap will be trounced, and vice versa. Take, for example, the 1990s. During the period between 1990 and 2000, large-cap stock outpaced small caps by an average of 6.6 percent per year. In the following decade, between 2000 and 2010, returns on small-cap stocks exceeded large-cap stocks by approximately 4.5 percent per annum. These are significant, and applying the wrong benchmark may drive someone to underestimate or overestimate the performance of the investment in question.

There are some benchmarks that are inherently more problematic than others. Take the Dow Jones Industrial Average (DJIA), for example. Unlike the S&P 500, the DJIA is comprised of only thirty stocks and represents only 29 percent of the value of US stocks as opposed to 89 percent by the S&P 500. Which stocks are included is fairly arbitrary (e.g., Microsoft but not Google or Apple, which are larger in size). It is price-weighted rather than size-weighted, which means that the most expensive stocks (not those with the largest market caps) will have more weighting in the index. This doesn't make any sense. Ken Fisher provides us with a dramatic example of this. If Microsoft, which is three times larger than 3M, has a share price that is one-third of 3M's share price, it will have only one-third the weighting of 3M. [26] The logic of this system escapes me.

On a final note, all performance comparisons should be done net of all fees and sales charges. This includes all management fees, consulting fees, custody fees, and transaction fees. Oftentimes, managers or financial institutions provide performance results on a gross basis, which is profoundly misleading. Always confirm with your investment managers, brokers, and advisors that performance is net of all fees. If it is not, ask them to adjust their reporting going forward and provide you with only the net return to your portfolio.

Not Everything Measurable Is Meaningful

Just as it is important to know what should be measured, it is of equal importance to know what should not be. We can measure outcomes and past performance, but that doesn't mean it is meaningful. It is important to remember that just because there is a metric attached to an opportunity or asset, it does not mean this number is necessarily relevant to our investment decisions. I will spare you the countless examples of ratios and metrics used by Wall Street to justify the salaries of spreadsheet wizards who have not made any money for their clients, but suffice it to say that something may be measurable in the short term but completely irrelevant over the long term and vice versa. Charley Ellis has analogized this phenomenon to Heisenberg's principle of indeterminacy that states that one cannot simultaneously measure the momentum and position of a particle. Being precise about one will automatically mean being imprecise about the other. The same can be said about measuring short-term and long-term investment results. The two are often mutually exclusive.

There is no shortage of data suggesting that even the best performers have down years, and virtually all top-quartile funds over a ten-year period have at least one year where they find themselves in the lowest quartile.[27] For these reasons, volatility can be an extraneous measure for someone who cares about the long-term success of a business, much as bond-trading prices may be immaterial to someone who is holding a bond to maturity.

Although some metrics are meaningless in the context of your particular IPS, they may be taken advantage of for your benefit. As we have already said, volatility and liquidity are the easiest risks to get paid for and the two most overrated risks for investors with sufficient cash reserves (i.e., no imminent need to access their capital).

If a company is throwing off sufficient cash, has a healthy balance sheet, and good prospects in the market, what difference does it make what the market prices are at today? It only matters if you have to sell it today, and that is where planning becomes critical. If all the right safeguards can be imposed, then volatility and liquidity can be easily endured and provide the portfolio with the prospect of higher returns.

Comfort as Measure of Performance

There is one metric, irrespective of its relevance that needs to be duly considered and even accommodated. That is the metric of comfort.

One of the most important ways of measuring performance and even risk is for a "sleep-at-night" quotient. This is the point where you do not worry about your investments and can sleep at night. If you are one of the few who is fortunate to have substantial net worth, it is truly a blessing. If that net worth causes you anxiety, sleep deprivation, and unease, you have taken what should be a blessing and made it into a curse. Bond king Bill Gross advises investors, "Sell to the sleeping point. If you lie awake at nights worrying about your investments, you own too much or are taking too much risk."[28] Notably, stress and anxiety have been proven to deteriorate the quality of decisions. In many instances chronic stress leads to tunnel vision, whose implications lead to more chronic stress. It is important to take time to check yourself in this area. Life is too short to spend it worrying about investing. No one should lose sight of that, and if you cannot do it yourself, find someone who can help settle your nerves and allow you to enjoy the prosperity you are privileged to have.

There are countless databases showcasing funds that have outperformed the benchmark, but there is no database of the right-fitting investment opportunities that will provide you the peace of mind you need to enjoy the more important things in life. That is why having a proper advisor or consultant at your side who can provide a healthy dose of perspective on every investment in every market cycle is invaluable for both the portfolio and one's quality of life.

Personal Performance Review

Now that you have a sense of how to think about performance, benchmarks, streaks, and even the role of luck, what remains is how to assess yourself and your trusted advisors.* At what point should you do your own performance review? How long will it take for you to realize the fruits of your labors? And what are some of the pitfalls to avoid?

Your performance review does not refer to the performance of individual managers or how often you rebalanced. It is about looking for objective assessments of your and your advisor's work on the portfolio as a whole.

The first concern is that we tend to overrate ourselves both from the point of view of past performance and the likelihood of future performance. Researchers have found that all individuals overstate their personal returns. This is true when other people are managing their money, but it is even truer when people make their own decisions.[29] For example, I have individuals come to my office with portfolios where they believe consistently outperform the market. After a simple calculation of the internal rate of return across all their positions, it becomes clear that the opposite has been true all along.

On top of overestimating our performance, people tend to employ a hindsight bias, where what is originally believed or aspired to is distorted. This bias makes returns a moving target and difficult to compare.

---

* This question is particularly germane to investors that manage their own affairs or are involved in the decision-making of their overall portfolio. This would be in contrast to those who hand off all their money to one discretionary advisor or money manager (which, in my humble opinion, is irresponsible).

This problem of overestimating performance can be mitigated by employing a third-party consultant or advisor who can assist with objectively measuring performance. (Caveat: Be prepared to be disappointed.) To combat hindsight bias, go back to the IPS and make sure adherence to it is rigorous, and make sure to reference it whenever reviewing annual performance numbers.

Time Horizon

The biggest challenge that most investors face in conducting effective personal reviews of their portfolios is the lack of understanding of what is a sufficient time horizon. It is important to ask, at what point in time can goals reasonably be expected to be met? The answer to this question may very well be the least palatable insight I share throughout the book, but I believe that it will take anywhere from five to ten years to demonstrate that a properly diversified portfolio has achieved exactly what was intended. Institutional investors intuitively understand this fact, and it certainly helps that some of them have nearly infinite time horizons. However, private investors, who have become accustomed to the almost instant liquidity and minute-to-minute measurements of public markets have a hard time with this investment horizon.

Having a five- to ten-year time horizon does not mean that you are not meeting and gauging your goals along the way, nor should a longer time horizon ever justify bad decisions in the short term. You should certainly be covering your expenditures, and the asset classes should be achieving results that are somewhere in line with their dynamic or relative benchmarks, along with both liquidity and asset allocation targets in the IPS. However, we will not necessarily achieve our absolute benchmark—which is most important—with less than five to seven years of runway. And often even five years may be too tight; seven to ten years is ideal.

There are multiple reasons for this. For starters, the types of assets that provide true diversification to a portfolio (e.g., private equity or real assets) do not generally provide short-term liquidity. If it is a development project or a turnaround company, it may be a few years before the assets are even cash-flowing. Investing in value where others don't readily see it often requires time for the facts to come to light or results to crystalize. That is the nature of these asset classes. To get exposure to them, one must play by different rules than public equities but, if played properly, should be generously compensated for the illiquidity. Richard Thaler goes so far as to say that "the attractiveness of a risky asset depends on the time horizon of the investor. An investor who is prepared to wait a long time before evaluating the outcome of the investment as a gain or a loss will find the risky asset more attractive than another who expects to evaluate the outcome soon."[30]

Being opportunistic with allocations also plays an important role in time lines. If someone walked into my office tomorrow and asked me to help him allocate his portfolio of $50 million immediately, I would probably make no more than a few starting allocations; the rest would have to sit and wait for high-conviction opportunities to present themselves. Undoubtedly those opportunities will come, but the most compelling ones are rarely available on demand. This gradual and opportunistic allocation process requires time.

Lastly, any three-year period can be skewed by unusual events. For example, in the credit crisis of 2008, no one was fully immunized. Everyone who had any type of exposure to financial markets felt a pinch. Even properly diversified investors had some drawdowns that year.* In fact, in the three-year period culminating in 2008, very few investors would have met their absolute benchmark. However, because extraordinary times also present extraordinary opportunities, having another year or two will often allow truly diversified portfolios to prove their worth.

---

* For example, my clients' properly diversified portfolios experienced single-digit or low double-digit drawdowns in 2008, as compared to the S&P 500, which experienced 40 percent drawdowns for the year.

It is common knowledge that every great enterprise requires pain in the short term to achieve excellence in the long term. By the time Tiger Woods was twenty-one, he had won four of the fifteen PGA Tour tournaments he had entered and had dominated the Masters by a record-breaking twelve strokes. Yet despite these remarkable feats, upon review of the videotapes, Woods concluded that his "swing really sucks." He enlisted his coach, Butch Harmon, to help him change his swing. Changing a swing was no small commitment, however. In all likelihood, it would mean getting worse in the near future to get better down the road. While his swing improved in both power and accuracy, he only won one tour event from July 1997 to February 1999. Despite what the statistics said, Woods claimed that he was a better golfer. The payoff finally came in the spring of 1999. That year, Woods won ten of the next fourteen events and eight PGA Tour events. In 2000, he had another nine PGA Tour wins, and after winning the 2001 Masters, he became the first golfer to win all four majors simultaneously.[31]

Results are not instantaneous, and investments may require short-term dips. In fact, most value investors will tell you that almost every time they buy an undervalued company, the stock plummets further before continuing to realize its market value. Over an investment time horizon, however, value investors have proven time and again to outperform the masses.

The biggest challenge with long-term investing is that it is somewhat unnatural. Researcher Robert Sapolsky contends that our evolutionary makeup is one that's adaptable to short-term threats. If we see a predator, we run. That is our physiological constitution and response. That is the reason why when seeing short-term losses, we may perceive them as a threat and run even when we would be safer if we stayed put.[32] Similarly, it has been found that human beings are terrible at delaying gratification. If given the choice, most people would prefer to receive $100 today than $150 dollars a year from now, despite the fact that most would be thrilled to have gotten a 50 percent return on their capital.[33]

At the very least, humans like to have robust feedback loops to let them know that they are on the right path. In long-term investments, however, there is often a weak feedback loop. In fields such as meteorology, medicine, or physics, feedback loops allow us to assess and refine our original assumptions, improve the formula, and improve predictability. Investing, however, is infinitely more complex and the feedback look is far weaker. The many variables can rarely be isolated in a laboratory environment, so it is difficult to identify any one point to improve or modify. Investing is more like raising children, where today's actions have consequences a decade from now, but you don't know exactly what will have the most profound impact and what will be forgotten. Much like parenting, there are clear dos and don'ts in investing, but hourly swings in sentiment are poor indicators of how well a child will mature.

This should be remembered by those who are constantly monitoring the market and making regular changes to their portfolios (i.e., short-term investors), and who believe they are receiving feedback upon which they could quickly assess or reassess their premises and modify their course of action. Short-term feedback is alluring, but it is often independent of any thesis and may simply be a symptom of the market's sentimental vagaries. This means that this perceived feedback may inhibit the staying power investors need to weather the inevitable, yet transient, storms of the markets. The role of a worthy advisor is to keep the ship steady when the waters are rough, ensuring that investors focus on fundamentals and don't confuse the signal with the noise.

An appropriate closing metaphor on the topic can be found in the growth pattern of the Chinese bamboo plant. Unlike most trees, Chinese bamboo is planted, watered, and nurtured for an entire season. Yet after all this care, nothing but a tiny shoot is seen. The next season, the farmer emerges again, irrigating, fertilizing, and tending to the bamboo plant, and yet again nothing sprouts. The farmer repeats this seemingly fruitless exercise for a third year, again without a product to show for it. By year four, he is surely criticized by friends and family members for his wasted efforts, and yet he persists to care for this minuscule shoot. Just when our farmer is about to give up, in the fifth year, the Chinese bamboo tree surges some eighty feet. Whether it comes to our children, our businesses, our friends, or our investments, everything meaningful in life takes time. It may take four years for something to mature, without more than a humble bud to show above the surface. But with patience, one will reap the benefits. If the farmer dug up those seeds each year to see where they stood, he would have undoubtedly compromised the foundation that allows for bamboo's extraordinary growth. The same is true in investing. Prospective clients I meet with that don't readily get this long-term approach often say, "Isn't that taking on too big of a risk? I have to experiment with this for seven years before I know that your advice worked?" The reality is that they will have to wait that long to fully realize the fruits of their labor, but it takes much less time to witness progress and intuitively feel that the process is essential for best-practice investing.

With all this said about long-term growth, it should be said that this is not advice for people who want to save their money because they may need their capital tomorrow. For savers, deploying capital in anything other than money market funds or certificates of deposits is probably imprudent. If, however, you are an investor, accept the fact that you are in it for the long term and act accordingly.

KEY TAKEAWAYS FROM PART V

- Beware of investment "stars" whose past performance was based on luck and has no bearing on future performance.
- Because no one can perfectly predict the movements of stocks either upwards or downwards, investing in public securities always involves some measure of luck. This can make differentiating between luck and skill difficult.
- To statistically confirm that skill rather than luck was involved would require a longer time horizon than most of us have. Long streaks do, however, suggest the presence of exceptional skills.
- Process—doing the right things, at the right times, and for the right reason—is more important than short-term outcomes.
- The most important benchmarks for private investors are those tailored to their needs and determined by intelligent asset allocation. These benchmarks are static.
- Various indices (e.g., S&P 500) are used to help assess the performance of underlying asset classes or managers within the portfolio. These benchmarks are dynamic.
- Not everything that's measureable is meaningful. So comfort or peace of mind can sometimes be the most valuable benchmark.

PART VI

THE EXPECTATIONS

Money is a terrible master, but an excellent servant.

—P.T. Barnum

After having spent most of this book discussing what we should expect from individuals—advisors, money managers, and ourselves—it is best to conclude this conversation with some thoughts on what we can expect from the financial industry as a whole and the environment in which we will be making investment decisions.

Performance Expectations

In his book *Full House: The Spread of Excellence from Plato to Darwin*, Stephen Jay Gould highlights a fascinating evolutionary phenomenon in baseball. He notes that between the years of 1901 and 1930, there were nine seasons in which at least one batter had a batting average above .400. However, in the eighty years that followed, there was only one baseball player to exceed a .400 batting average, and that was Ted Williams, hitting .406 in 1941. Gould's hypothesis is that this is reflective of an ever more competitive landscape. The pitching became increasingly refined, the fielding became better every year, and the information about each player became more sophisticated.

The legendary investor, author, and economist Peter L. Bernstein adapted Gould's theory to money management.[1] In his 1998 article in *Financial Analysts Journal*, "Where, Oh Where Are the .400 Hitters of Yesteryear?" Bernstein asserts that the same phenomenon Gould described in baseball was taking shape in the equity markets. He claimed that as a result of ever-increasing levels of knowledge, education, financial sophistication, and information (not to mention computing power), the odds of stardom and exceptional performance would diminish. He even points to Warren Buffett, whose performance, albeit consistently positive, was on a gradual decline. Indeed, Buffett posted larger returns in the 1960s and 1970s than he did in the 1980s and 1990s, and his returns from 2000 to 2020 will likely diminish even further. Invariably, limited outperformance translates into a great deal more average performance. Bernstein agreed and pointed to his data that showed that between 1960 and 1997 there was a gradual and progressive decline in the standard deviations of mutual funds.

Bernstein fortified his argument by demonstrating that since 1984, the top quintile of fund managers beat the S&P 500 by a narrower margin than in the past while the bottom quintile performers lagged by margins as great as, or even greater than, before. Effectively, there continues to be greater efficiency in the market and investment managers are now playing it safe. They are avoiding the large swings of concentrated portfolios, and as a consequence, they aren't adjusting position sizes to be commensurate with their most attractive opportunities (i.e., with the best ideas getting the most capital). This, in turn, translates into mediocrity, and the cycle continues.

In addition, there is the speed of today's commercial activity that make finding investments harder than ever before. Innovation is exploding at a rapid pace. Product development times are shrinking. Large companies can get bitten by small players more quickly than ever before. Competitors imitate almost instantly, and new kings take the hill at an ever-increasing pace.[2] In the 1980s, most calculations were still done manually, while in the 2000s, computers are analyzing extraordinary volumes of data instantaneously. All these factors make inefficiencies, mispricing, or arbitrage opportunities more difficult to find and capitalize on for any sustained period of time. As the Hunt brothers* can testify, even in the slower-paced days of the 1970s, market manipulation proved unlikely. Today, it is nearly impossible.

Charles Ellis echoes these sentiments and points to the gradual disappearance of day traders, along with the trend of the largest institutions doing an even larger share of the trading. The market shifted from only 10 percent of NYSE dollars being invested by institutions to 90 percent (50 percent of all trading activity coming from the fifty largest institutions in the market, and 75 percent by the hundred largest institutions), and as a result, the level of competition has increased dramatically, edging out nonprofessionals from the market. The individuals at these large institutions are among the brightest, most educated, highly motivated, hardworking, and competitive professionals out there. They are looking for every mistake anyone in the market makes in order to jump on it and capitalize on it. This means that when a private investor makes a trade from his or her two-person family office, the party on the other side may be a Goldman Sachs, Bank of America, or Berkshire Hathaway. Who do you think has the informational edge in that transaction? With their remarkably deep pockets and massive investments in research and technology, these institutional investors are now more sophisticated than ever before, competing in a more transparent and rapid market.

Ellis turns to scientist Simon Ramo for a brilliant analogy about the difference between professional investors and nonprofessional

---

* In an effort to control the global silver market, billionaire brothers Nelson and William Hunt began buying up silver, using a fair bit of leverage in the process. The scheme reached a crescendo when the brothers acquired over two hundred million ounces of silver, exceeding half of all the deliverable silver in the world at the time. In one year's time, the price of silver shot up from ten dollars to fifty dollars per ounce. What the brothers neglected to consider is basic economics. Higher demand translates into greater supply. The silver bubble prompted people to melt down their jewelry, tea sets, and anything else they could get their hands one. With the market flooded by silver, the price collapsed back to ten dollars an ounce, and the brothers were forced to sell everything to meet margin calls and quickly found themselves in bankruptcy.

investors. Ramo pointed out that in tennis there are actually two different games—one game played by professionals and one game played by everyone else. Professionals play hard and with precision, using strategies to outmaneuver their opponents. The outcome is determined by the winner. In amateur tennis, however, the goal is usually to just stay alive, and the game is determined by the loser—the one who messes up more often.[3] Ellis suggests that this is what investment management has become; it has evolved from a winner's game to a loser's game as a result of the market becoming dominated by institutional investors.[4]

The bottom line is that going forward performance expectations in public markets must be kept low. Expect your larger managers to have a more difficult time making money, and craft your IPS accordingly.

The Challenges of Size and Success

Investment managers often become big because they are successful. Once they are too big, however, they often plateau and sometimes even jeopardize their stellar record of outperformance. A great example of this phenomenon is Bill Miller's Legg Mason Value Trust fund. By 2005, Legg Mason was the hottest mutual fund in the United States after having beaten the S&P 500 index for fifteen consecutive years. At the time, no other fund in the previous forty years had had such a long streak of outperformance, and it was the best-performing mutual fund in US history. Given what we have said about streaks, it is almost statistically impossible that exceptional skill was absent from the equation, and this made the fund even more tantalizing. There was a flash flood of new money; it came in faster than Bill Miller could deploy it. But after this gush of cash, Miller's performance began to lag, and with additional funds, it went from bad to worse. Between 2006 and 2011, with one exception, Miller had underperformed the market every year. He resigned from the fund in 2012.

Miller realized that size had contributed to his downfall, and he regrouped to run a new fund called Legg Mason Opportunity Trust that had less than 10 percent of the AUM that had come to his previous fund. Naturally, this fund was the best-performing mutual fund in 2012 with a return of 40 percent.[5]

Commenting on the impact of his large asset bases, Miller said in an interview that it is "mathematically true" that there is a portfolio size "beyond which it is difficult, if not impossible, to beat the market."[6] Indeed, being small has remarkable competitive advantages. It means being nimble and able to respond to minor dislocations— which will always exist. Whether in investing or any other realm of life, the biggest and strongest are not necessarily the most effective. In his book *David and Goliath*, Malcolm Gladwell describes how T. E. Lawrence (a.k.a. Lawrence of Arabia) led a small, untrained, and barely armed militia to victory against the formidable Turkish army, which controlled the Arabian Peninsula at that time. Gladwell also points out that in all the wars fought over the last two hundred years, the weaker country has defeated the stronger and far superior army some 30 percent of the time. In fact, if the weaker country employed an unconventional war strategy, they defeated the stronger army over 63 percent of the time.[7] Size presents some opportunities for the small that are unavailable to the large.

Jack Bogle, the founder of Vanguard and indexing advocate, has often called into question the ability of large active managers to add value, saying: "Those who make lots of acquisitions for the sake of growth or the investment manager who collects lots of AUM will find it more difficult to add value as the size of the enterprise swells." Bogle notes how profoundly a manager's investment options become limited as assets grow. This is evident in public equities where the investable universe of stocks declines sharply as funds increase in size. Assuming that a fund can hold no more than 5 percent of the outstanding shares of any company, Bogle estimates that a fund with $1 billion of assets can choose from over 1,900 stocks while a fund with

$20 billion has a universe of about 250 stocks. So it happens that success can sow the seeds of its own failure.[8]

Size is not a challenge solely for money managers. All companies experience slowdowns upon reaching a certain level of scale. Studies have shown that the fifty largest companies between 1980 and 2006 underperformed the S&P 500 over one-, three-, and five-year periods.[9] In addition, research by the Corporate Strategy Board found that large companies experience growth stalls when they reach the $20 billion to $30 billion range.[10]

The challenges of size are readily obvious to the wisest investors in the business, and some of them actually use size as a cue that it's time to pull down the curtain. One of the most notable examples is Stanley Druckenmiller's closure of Duquesne Capital Management. For thirty years, Druckenmiller ran Duquesne with a staggering performance of approximately 30 percent per annum, without a single down year, returning 11 percent even in 2008. These numbers are virtually unmatched in the business. Duquesne did not take in any new investors for over a decade, so most of the growth in the $12 billion portfolio came from performance. In August of 2010, however, Druckenmiller told clients that he found managing such an enormous amount of capital too difficult and that it would impose on him the stress of performing in a way that he would deem to be disappointing.[11] He then closed the fund.

Notably, this is the very same reason Druckenmiller left George Soros, his partner in the Quantum Fund. He claimed that Quantum's size "was having a clear impact on my ability to perform, as well as my state of being." For someone who can be counted among the greatest investors of all time to claim size as the most significant motivation for exiting both funds is telling. And his story is not unique. Many others, some among the world's greatest investment managers, have chosen to return capital or retire when they simply couldn't match their asset base to the most compelling opportunities that they were finding. Thomas Rowe Price, founder of T. Rowe Price, left his own firm when he felt his organization had moved beyond its capacity to produce outsized returns on a go-forward basis. Most recently, in the fall of 2013, Seth Klarman's Baupost Group, which was among the largest and most successful hedge funds in the world, announced that it is returning capital for the same reason.

In the business of money management, returning capital is counterintuitive. It requires making the conscious decision to take a lesser paycheck so that your clients do not have to settle for lower returns than those they have been spoiled with. But this counterintuition (i.e., putting shareholders' interests ahead of personal compensation) is the very reason for these individuals' successes. It is counterintuitive to sell your winners and buy your losers. It is counterintuitive to sit on your hands when valuations are approaching historic heights. But these are the ingredients—along with size management—that allow legendary investment managers to achieve unparalleled returns.

Regrettably, in most pockets of the industry, the exact opposite is occurring. The large players are getting larger at the expense of their clients. The small players, who are best able to extract the most value for their clients, are either being eaten up by the larger ones (and joining the merry party of mediocrity) or suffocating under the onerous burden of regulatory compliance—further exacerbating the prospect of lower returns.

The Investor's Advantage

There are countless people on Wall Street or in any financial center around the world that have more technical knowledge than you do. There are countless individuals with better math skills and more time or talent devoted to it than you ever will. Your odds of outsmarting these massive institutions are equal to my odds of me beating LeBron James one-on-one. You may not have seen me play basketball, but rest assured the odds are stacked against me, and your odds of outsmarting the wizards of Goldman Sachs, Morgan Stanley, and Citigroup are not good.

Fortunately, investing has various components. There are the intellectual elements (technical knowledge), the physical elements (immense research resources), and psychological elements (sentiments of the masses). The psychological realm is where you can establish a firm advantage.

Over the past fifty years, the average holding period for a stock went down from eight years to five days.[12] The world has become impatient. And in a world where a prank on Twitter can clip $136.5 billion off the S&P 500,[13] irrelevant information is making investors more irrational. This trend is compounded by the explosive growth of exchange-traded funds, which research suggests have only exacerbated the volatility and impulsiveness of the market.[14] Markets operate according to the dictates of chaos theory, where small and unpredictable forces can produce disproportionately large reactions. And it is in this environment, where few people are able to go against their emotional grain, that volatility has earned a seat in the pantheon of investor preoccupations.

When performance is measured every quarter, every month, every day, or even every time clients check their brokerage accounts, long-term perspectives and emotional stability to ride out temporary fluctuations is in short supply. But this means that those individuals with forbearance can achieve what even the largest institutions cannot. One of the greatest private investors in history, Warren Buffett, has a preferred holding period of forever and checks with management only once or twice a year. If he was wrong about his assessment of a company, Buffett will cut his losses (as he has done on countless occasions), but for his highest conviction ideas, the exit is "forever" away because he knows that any enterprise of meaning takes time to develop and one silly Tweet should not unravel it.

By being patient, mastering the best practices of investment decisions, understanding the industry, and having proper counsel at your side, you will give yourself a high probability of achieving your financial goals. By overcoming various behavioral biases and adhering to a disciplined process when markets are dominated by turmoil, panic, and fear, you will have the psychological advantage.

As a private investor, you need not worry about career risk* or looking foolish to anyone but yourself. You have the flexibility to own just about anything and are not limited to securities of any size. You can enter or exit a position without impacting markets. There are no high-frequency traders trying to pick off your orders, no public scrutiny of your holdings, and no need to inform the Securities and Exchange Commission of every decision.[15] So, while the challenges of successfully investing capital have never been greater, neither have the structural and psychological advantages of the more nimble private investor.

Closing Thoughts

There are both challenges and advantages to procuring proper investment advice for those who are focused on capital preservation. There is a pervasive culture of salesmanship, rather than stewardship, in the industry that makes finding a trusted advisor the first and most difficult decision an investor will face. This will also be the first of many times that an investor will need to take action in order to hold onto the capital he or she has built. At the very least, investors need to come to the table with a willingness to educate themselves, the strength of independence (to make decisions that are uniquely right for them), and a good dose of humility (to admit when they need

---

* Career risk is an economist's term for people who operate on behalf of others—and as a result of insecurity over their jobs or simply looking foolish, they are more conservative or act more conventionally and take less risk than they may need to take. John Maynard Keynes described this complex by saying, "It's better to fail conventionally then succeed unconventionally."

help). But beyond these soft skills, there is a lot of planning, sourcing, researching, selecting, monitoring, and rebalancing that needs to be done, and no one with substantial capital should tackle this on his or her own. A good advisor will help navigate the challenges and obstacles out there, many of which I have mentioned in this book. There are issues surrounding compensation and fees and their impact on decisions; there are performance measurements and how they help or hinder properly assessing specific investments and a portfolio as a whole; and there is navigating the psychological minefield of determining what is luck and what is skill and how both factor into your decisions.

Throughout this book, I have set a fairly high bar for the investment advisory industry. A high standard is achievable and available, but unfortunately, it is not commonly met because it requires advisors to do more work and get paid less than what the industry has offered in the past. Further, the interests of clients are often at odds with those of the shareholders of a firm (e.g., the higher the clients' fees, the better it is for the firm but the worse for the client). Indeed, as someone who has spent years building a firm that is committed to living up to the standards outlined thus far, I can tell you that it is not a simple endeavor. Over the years, we have received our fair share of criticism from other advisors, saying that our "business model doesn't make sense," that "no one will buy us," or that we "weren't being realistic," but we stuck to our values and have a robust firm and grateful clients to show for it.

Despite our own successes, it is not a common dynamic in the industry, and when I set out to write this book, I struggled with how to advise investors. If I were to outline an optimal dynamic between investors and advisors, it would be removed from where most advisors find themselves today, and most investors would have difficulty accessing advisors of this caliber. At the same time, if I set the bar of expectation lower than where it ought to be, then I would be selling you short of what is possible and optimal for you as an affluent investor. I chose not to sell you short.

Even if the advisor you have is not meeting this standard, at bare minimum, ensure that he or she is capable of shining light on what you do not see, plays devil's advocate for viable alternatives, and helps manage your biases to avoid detrimental mistakes.

In 2005, there was a fascinating study conducted by distinguished social psychologist Richard E. Nisbett. In this study, Nisbett showed both American and Chinese students a series of fairly pedestrian images (e.g., a car on the road, a tiger in the forest, a plane in the sky) while measuring their every squint, eye movement, and focus of attention. It was quickly apparent to Nisbett that these two groups were looking at the same pictures in profoundly different ways. The American students focused almost exclusively on the focal point (i.e., the car, the tiger, the plane), whereas the Chinese students focused primarily on the background (i.e., the sun, the clouds, the leaves, the sand), taking much longer to zero in on the focal point. This meant that if there was a pothole behind the car or a snake not far from the tiger, the Chinese student would notice it and the American would not.[16] Investing, like any other important decisions we make, requires seeing both the essence of what is in front of you and the context in which it is found. We should be aware that our experiences, predilections, and cultural traits lead us to focus on certain aspects of investing, perhaps missing important aspects of the story. The role of any trusted advisor is first and foremost to fill those gaps and to show you what you are not seeing. That is the reason Warren Buffett is the only CEO in America that invites short sellers of Berkshire Hathaway to his annual general meeting.[17] He knows that his investing decisions will be better informed when challenged by others.

The blind spots we all have go beyond our cultural biases and into our cultural limitations. We live busy lives with hectic schedules and limited attention spans. But being busy does not mean that we have evolved into better multitaskers. We are still capable of focusing on only one thing at a time. In a study at the University of Washington, the researchers sent out a man dressed up as a clown to ride around the university campus on a unicycle. Notably, when he rode in front of individuals who were on their cell phones, the vast majority of them did not see him.[18] We can replace the cell phone with any other aspect in our lives—be it familial, professional, communal, or recreational. Studies suggest that there are only about 2 percent of the population who can truly do more than one thing at a time, and even they are prone to errors.[19] For the rest of us, we have to accept that we are prone to tunnel vision and have many important items vying for our attention. The fact is that investing is a means to an end, but it is certainly not the end in and of itself, and it should not be where we spend most of our limited ability to focus. The most valuable assets in life are those that have no defined values on our balance sheets, such as our family, friends, health, and many other passions or preoccupations. No one can juggle everything, but everyone can prioritize their lives to focus on the most important things, especially those intangibles that make life worth living. That is why it is imperative to have someone who can help you focus on your nest egg, ensuring mistakes are avoided and the capital is preserved. Investment advice is one-fifth asset management and four-fifths behavior management. Along with all the other traits we have discussed, make sure your advisor embodies this belief and helps you sidestep the biases, cultural tendencies, and irrational behavior we are all guilty of from time to time. Then and only then will you be in the best position to achieve excellence in the management of your wealth. And then you will know you have a true partner in preservation.

KEY TAKEAWAYS FROM PART VI

- The investment landscape is becoming more competitive. This means that returns will be more difficult to achieve and even the most renowned investors will see diminished returns.
- On the up side, new technology and innovation will continue to create opportunities, making the broadest spectrum of investments more accessible.
- The increasing sizes of today's top performers will likely dampen their future returns, as outsized assets almost invariably limit the prospects of outsized returns.
- Individual investors have many advantages over well-endowed institutional investors. Individual investors don't need to worry about career risk or size constraints, and they have the freedom to ignore the market's volatility by not needing to manage towards quarter-end or year-end numbers.
- Investing requires seeing both what's in front of you and the context in which it is found. The role of the advisor is to fill in the gaps and blind spots we all have.
- The standards laid out in this book are high but achievable.
- Given that investing is one-fifth asset management and four-fifths behavior management, ensure that your advisor can manage (both your and his) behavior to help you make better investment decisions.

APPENDIX

INVESTMENT ADVISOR CHECKLIST

To simplify the numerous suggestions provided throughout the book, I wanted to provide you with a checklist that may help you in your selection of the ideal partner in preservation. Please note that very few advisors will have all these characteristics, but whoever you are considering should possess at least the majority of the qualities (and avoid the majority of shortcomings) outlined below.

- Does the advisor have depth of both knowledge and experience in advising high-net-worth investors? (Reminder: Ignore the designation.)
- Does the advisor aid in the construction of a robust IPS?
- Does the advisor put process ahead of product or vice versa?
- Does the advisor take an aggressive directional view vis-à-vis the market?
- Does the advisor have access to the broadest range of assets classes?
- Does the advisor have the capacity to research and identify best-in-class investment opportunities?
- Can the advisor tailor all those opportunities to your specific needs?
- Does the advisor have a robust understanding of the investment universe and have a firm grasp of financial history?
- Does the advisor challenge your thinking or merely follow your lead?
- Does the advisor recognize the various biases investors are subject to and work to ensure you are not entrapped by them?
- Does the advisor have proprietary products that would make him or her biased in what you do or do not invest in?
- Is the advisor's compensation aligned with your interests?

- Is all compensation fully disclosed before the start of the working relationship?
- Does the compensation incentivize the advisor to push any behavior on you (i.e., invest more, trade more, take more risk, etc.)?
- Does the advisor truly concern himself or herself with your full financial picture—cash flow, estate plan, and so on?
- Does the advisor monitor and fully consider your liquidity needs?
- Does the advisor liaise with other advisors (accountants, lawyers, etc.) to ensure that all investment decisions are truly holistic and strategic?
- Is the advisor attempting to add value to you at every turn?
- How does the advisor measure the value he or she brings to you?
- Is the entire portfolio's performance calculated and reported (after fees)?
- Is benchmarking conducted in a consistent, thoughtful, and disciplined fashion?
- Does the advisor recognize the roles of luck and skill in investing?
- Does the advisor sufficiently consider frequent reversions to the mean?
- Is the prescribed asset allocation maintained by adherence to routine rebalancing?
- Does your advisor allow you to sleep well at night?
- Is the advisor committed to continuous improvement?

NOTES & REFERENCES

Introduction

1. D. Dorn and P. Sengmueller, "Trading as Entertainment?" *Management Science 55*, no. 4 (2009): 591–603, http://faculty. lebow.drexel.edu/dornd/te.pdf. The authors suggest that sensation seekers and those who trade for entertainment purposes tend to churn portfolios at a higher rate and effectively diminish returns.

Part I: Investment Advice

1. G. Lubin, "The 13 Richest Americans of All Time," *Business Insider*, April 17, 2011, http://www.businessinsider.com/richest-americans-ever-2011-4?op=1.

2. "Richest Americans in History," *Forbes*, August 24, 1998, http://www.forbes.com/asap/1998/0824/032.html.

3. A. T. Vanderbilt, II, *Fortune's Children: The Fall of the House of Vanderbilt* (New York: William Morrow / HarperCollins, 2001), 1803.

4. M. Sullivan, "Lost Inheritance," *Wall Street Journal*, March 8, 2013, http://www.wsj.com/articles/SB100014241278873246624045783346632711139552.

5. "Almost 80 percent of National Football League players are flirting with bankruptcy two years after they retire, according to *Sports Illustrated*. NBA players aren't faring much better. Sixty percent of former National Basketball Association players end up broke within five years of retirement." See M. Riddix, "Seven Costly Pro Athlete Screw-Ups," Yahoo Sports, March 10, 2010, https://ca.sports. yahoo.com/top/news?slug=ys-investopediamoneyloss031010.

6. "The National Endowment for Financial Education points to research that estimates 70 per cent of people who unexpectedly come into large sums of money will lose it within seven years." See C. Commisso, "Why Most Lottery Winners End Up Losing Their

New Fortune," CTVNews.ca, March 26, 2013, http://www.
ctvnews.ca/business/why-most-lottery-winners-end-up-losing-their-
new-fortune-1.1211569#ixzz2oY8O1HZC.

7. Ipsos Reid / Canadian Securities Administrators (CSA), *CSA
Investor Index Survey* (Calgary, Alberta, Canada: Author, 2009),
https://www.securities-administrators.ca/uploadedFiles/General/
pdfs/CSA%20Investor%20Index%202009%20Final_EN.pdf?n
=6519.

8. For further discussion of the CFM study, see Ipsos Reid, *Investor
Research: The Value of Advice* (Calgary, Alberta, Canada: Author,
2010), http://www.ci.com/web/pdf/ific_value_of_advice_e.pdf. It is
of course possible that the benefits we have outlined here are a function of correlation, not causation. In other words, only individuals
with significantly more capital to invest will be proceed to engage
(or can even afford) paying for investment advice. While it is
unlikely that receiving counsel actually offers no financial benefits,
in the interest of being statistically honest, the possibility of pure
correlation should be noted.

9. Financial Industry Regulatory Authority (FINRA), "Understanding Investment Professional Designations," accessed November 8,
2012, http://www.finra.org/investors/professional-designations.

10. Financial Industry Regulatory Authority (FINRA), "Selecting
Investment Professionals," accessed November 8, 2012,
http://www.finra.org/investors/choosing-investment-professional.

11. "Financial adviser," *Wikipedia*, accessed July 23, 2013,
http://en.wikipedia.org/wiki/Financial_adviser.

12. Regarding admissions criteria, the IFSE website explicitly
says, "Admission into any of www.IFSE.ca's programs is open to
all individuals. There are no academic requirements for entering
the Investment Funds Program." See P. Banerjee, "How Easy Is It
to Become A Financial Advisor?" Where Does All My Money Go?,
April 2008, http://wheredoesallmymoneygo.com/how-easy-is-it-to-
become-a-financial-advisor/.

13. J. Zweig and M. Pilon, "Is Your Adviser Pumping Up His Credentials?" *Wall Street Journal*, October 16, 2010, http://online.wsj.com/article/SB10001424052748703927504575540582361440848.html.
14. Brondesbury Group, *Demand-Based Investor Education Study: What Canadian Investors Want to Know and How They Want to Learn* (Toronto, Ontario: Author, 2010).
15. Ipsos Reid / Canadian Securities Administrators (CSA), *CSA Investor Index Survey* (Calgary, Alberta, Canada: Author, 2009), https://www.securities-administrators.ca/uploadedFiles/General/pdfs/CSA%20Investor%20Index%202009%20Final_EN.pdf?n=6519.
16. Gregg, Kelly, Sullivan & Woolstencroft, *The Joint Standing Committee on Retail Investor Issues: Retail Investor Information Survey* (Toronto, Ontario, Canada: Strategic Counsel, 2009), http://www.osc.gov.on.ca/static/_/JSC/jsc_retail-investor-info-survey.pdf.
17. This phenomenon is indicated in the results from the most recent Canadian Securities Administrators surveys. See Canadian Securities Administrators / Autorités Canadiennes en Valeurs Mobilières (CSA/ACVM), *CSA Investor Index, 2012* (Montréal, Québec, Canada: Authors, 2012), accessed August 9, 2013, http://www.securities-administrators.ca/ investortools.aspx?id=1011.
18. E. Rempel, "Why Don't Most Financial Planners Plan Finances?" MillionDollarJourney, October 20, 2009, http://www.milliondollarjourney.com/why-don%E2%80%99t-most-financial-planners-plan-finances.htm.
19. Ibid.
20. J. Picerno, "Why This Year's Nobel Award In Economics Makes Perfect Sense," *The Capital Spectator*, October 22, 2013, http://www.capitalspectator.com/archives/2013/10/why_this_years.html.

21. L. Plevin, "In Bogle Family, It's Either Passive or Aggressive," *Wall Street Journal*, November 28, 2013, http://online.wsj.com/news/articles/SB1000142405270230333290 4579224351143883302.

22. Ecclesiastes 3:1 (Authorized [King James] Version).

23. Kent L. Womack, "Do Brokerage Analysts' Recommendations Have Investment Value?" *Journal of Finance* 51, no. 1 (1996): 137–167, http://www.jstor.org/stable/2329305.

24. J. Zweig, "The Intelligent Investor: Conflict of Interest? Moi?" *Wall Street Journal*, October 5, 2012, http://online.wsj.com/news/articles/SB10000872396390443493330 4578038811945287932.

25. D. B. Bergstresser, J. M. R. Chalmers, and P. Tufano, "Assessing the Costs and Benefits of Brokers in the Mutual Fund Industry" (working paper) (Cambridge, MA: Harvard University, 2004), accessed August 28, 2013, http://www.people.hbs.edu/ptufano/bbenefits_Nov2004.pdf.

26. A. Hackethal, M. Haliassos, and T. Jappelli, "Financial Advisors: A Case of Babysitters?" (CEPR discussion paper 7235) (London, UK: Centre for Economic Policy Research, 2009), http://www.voxeu.org/article/do-financial-advisors-improve-portfo-lio-performance.

27. S. Mullainathan, M. Nöth, and A. Schoar, "The Market for Financial Advice: An Audit Study" (NBER working paper 17929) (Cambridge, MA: National Bureau of Economic Research, 2012), http://scholar.harvard.edu/files/mullainathan/files/the_market_for_f inancial_advice_an_audit_study.pdf.

28. Z. Sharek, R. E. Schoen, and G. Loewenstein, "Bias in the Eval-uation of Conflict of Interest Policies," *Journal of Law Medicine & Ethics* 40, no. 2 (2012): 368–82, doi:10.1111/j.1748-720X.2012.00670, PubMed PMID: 22789052.

29. E. Pronin, D. Y. Lin, and L. Ross, "The Bias Blind Spot: Perceptions of Bias in Self Versus Others," *Personality and Social Psychology Bulletin* 28, no. 3 (2002): 369–381; E. Pronin, T. Gilovich, and L. Ross, "Objectivity in the Eye of the Beholder: Divergent Perceptions of Bias in Self Versus Others," *Psychological Review* 111, no. 3 (2004): 781–799, http://psp.sagepub.com/content/28/3/369.short.

30. J. Zweig, *Your Money and Your Brain: How the New Science of Neuroeconomics Can Help Make You Rich* (New York: Simon and Schuster, 2007), 59.

31. This principal has come to be known as Laplace's Demon. See P. Simon and M. F. de Laplace, *A Philosophical Essay on Probabilities*, trans. W. Truscott and F. L. Emory (Hoboken, NJ /London: John Wiley / Chapman Hall, 1902).

32. J. R. Graham, and C. R. Harvey, "Grading the Performance of Market Timing Newsletters," *Financial Analysts Journal* 53, no. 6 (1997): 54–66, https://faculty.fuqua.duke.edu/~charvey/Research/Published_Papers/P44_Grading_the_performance.pdf.

33. A. Malmquist and A. Rhodin, "Universitetsuppsats: Good from Far or Far from Good?: An Experimental Study on Financial Experts Forecasting Ability," LIBRIS, Seek, January 1, 2007, http://arc.hhs.se/download.aspx?MediumId=410.

34. "Betting on Investment Skill," RPS Seawright, Above the Market, November 8, 2013, http://rpseawright.wordpress.com/2013/11/08/betting-on-investment-skill/.

35. M. King, "Investments: Orlando Is the Cat's Whiskers of Stock Picking," *Guardian*, January 12, 2013, http://www.theguardian.com/money/2013/jan/13/investments-stock-picking/print; F. E. Allen, "Cat Beats Professionals at Stock Picking," *Wall Street Journal*, January 15, 2013, http://www.forbes.com/sites/frederickallen/2013/01/15/cat-beats-professionals-at-stock-picking/.

36. R. Ferri, "Any Monkey Can Beat The Market," *Forbes*, December 20, 2012, http://www.forbes.com/sites/rickferri/2012/12/20/any-monkey-can-beat-the-market/.

37. M. Twain, *The $30,000 Bequest and Other Stories, Oxford Mark Twain* (Oxford, UK: Oxford University Press, 1906).

38. I. Ben-David, J. Graham, and C. Harvey, "Managerial Miscalibration," *Quarterly Journal of Economics* 128, no. 4 (2013): 1547–1584, http://dx.doi.org/10.2139/ssrn.1640552.

39. D. F. "A Load of Old Rubbish? Garbage In, Garbage Out: Dustmen Make the Best Forecasts," *Economist*, November 27, 2010, http://www.economist.com/blogs/theworldin2011/2010/11/garbage_garbage_out_dustmen_make_best_forecasts.

40. C. Heath and D. Heath, *Decisive: How to Make Better Choices in Life and Work* (New York: Crown Business / Random House, 2014), 142.

41. Tom Arnold, John H. Earl Jr., and David S. North, "Are Cover Stories Effective Contrarian Indicators?" *Financial Analysts Journal* 63, no. 2 (2007): 70–75.

42. L. D. Brown, "Analyst Forecasting Errors and Their Implications for Security Analysis," *Financial Analysts Journal* 52, no. 1 (1996), http://ssrn.com/abstract=1125375.

43. B. Portnoy, *The Investor's Paradox: The Power of Simplicity in a World of Overwhelming Choice* (New York: St. Martin's Press, 2014), 31–32.

44. German Consumer Affairs Ministry, "Study of Evers and Jung," *Anforderungen an Finanzvermittler*, September 2008, cited in Synovate, *Consumer Market Study on Advice within the Area of Retail Investment Services—Final Report* (London: Author, 2011), 14, http://ec.europa.eu/consumers/rights/docs/investment_advice_study_en.pdf.

45. N. Hertz, *Eyes Wide Open: How to Make Smart Decisions in a Confusing World* (New York: Harper Collins, 2013), 83.

46. Edelman Insights, "Global Deck: 2013 Edelman Trust Barometer," 2013, http://www.slideshare.net/EdelmanInsights/global-deck-2013-edelman-trust-barometer-16086761,slide 13.

47. M. Harrington, "What Banks Can Learn from Cars," *Edelman Insights*, February 5, 2013, http://www.edelman.com/post/what-banks-can-learn-from-cars/.

48. A. Kindergan, "Family Investment Offices: When Do They Make Sense?" *Financialist*, April 25, 2013, http://www.thefinancialist.com/family-investment-offices-when-do-they-make-sense-bill-woodson/.

Part II: The Investor

1. N. D. Weinstein, "Unrealistic Optimism about Future Life Events," *Journal of Personality and Social Psychology* 39, no. 5 (1980): 806–820, http://dx.doi.org/10.1037/0022-3514.39.5.806.

2. T. Odean, "What I Know About How You Invest," paper presented at the Legg Mason Funds Management Investment Conference, Las Vegas, Nevada, 2003, http://latrobefinancialmanagement.com/Research/Money_Management/What%20I%20Know%20About%20How%20You%20Invest.pdf.

3. S. E. Taylor and J. D. Brown, "Illusion and Well-Being: A Social Psychological Perspective on Mental Health," *Psychological Bulletin* 103, no. 2 (1988): 193–210, accessed October 27, 2013, http://taylorlab.psych.ucla.edu/1988_Illusion%20and%20well-being_A%20social%20psychological%20perspective%20on%20mental%20health.pdf.

4. J. Zweig, "Did You Beat the Market?" *Fundamentalist*, January 1, 2000, 55–57, http://money.cnn.com/magazines/moneymag/money-magarchive/2000/01/01/271477/.

5. W. J. Bernstein, *The Investors Manifesto: Preparing for Prosperity, Armageddon, and Everything in Between* (Hoboken, NJ: John Wiley, 2012), 10–11.

6. G. Soros, *The Crisis of Global Capitalism* (New York: Public Affairs Press, 1998), 24.

7. Reference here is to the smoker study by Timothy C. Brock (1965). See T. C. Brock, "Commitment to Exposure as a Determinant of Information Receptivity," *Journal of Personality and Social Psychology* 2 (1965): 10–19, http://dx.doi.org/10.1037/h0022082.

8. J. Zweig, *Your Money and Your Brain: How the New Science of Neuroeconomics Can Help Make You Rich* (New York: Simon and Schuster, 2007), 159.

9. US Securities and Exchange Commission, *Study Regarding Financial Literacy Among Investors* (Washington, DC: Author, 2002), http://www.sec.gov/news/studies/2012/917-financial-literacy-study-part1.pdf.

10. M. E. Lagomasino, *Beating the Odds: Improving the 15 Percent Probability of Staying Wealthy* (New York: JP Morgan Private Bank, 2004).

11. J. VanDerhei, S. Holden, L. Alonso, and Employee Benefit Research Institute (EBRI). "401(k) Plan Asset Allocation, Account Balances, and Loan Activity in 2008," *EBRI Issue Brief* 335 (October 2009), http://www.ebri.org/pdf/briefspdf/EBRI_IB_10-2009_No335_K-Update.pdf.

12. S. R. Waite, *Quantum Investing* (New York: Texere, 2003), 129.

13. R. J. Shiller, *Irrational Exuberance.* (Princeton, NJ: Princeton University Press, 2000), 199–200.

14. J. M. Buchannan, *The Theory of Public Choice—II* (Ann Arbor, MI: University of Michigan, 1984), 262.

15. C. Ellis, *Winning the Loser's Game: Timeless Strategies for Successful Investing*, 4th edition (New York: McGraw-Hill, 2002), 142.

16. C. Heath and D. Heath, *Decisive: How to Make Better Choices in Life and Work* (New York: Crown Business / Random House, 2014), 17.

17. Barna Group. "Americans Describe Their Views about Life after Death," 2003, accessed November 12, 2013, https://www.barna.org/barna-update/article/5-barna-update/128-americans-describe-their-views-about-life-after-death#.UsD4QSfWs4Q.

18. B. M. Barber and T. Odean, "Boys Will Be Boys: Gender Over-confidence, and Common Stock Investment," *Quarterly Journal of Economics* 116, no. 1 (2001): 261–292.

19. K. L. Fisher and L. Hoffmans, *Debunkery: Learn It, Do It, and Profit from It—Seeing Through Wall Street's Money-Killing Myths* (Hoboken, NJ: Fisher Investments / John Wiley, 2011), 74.

20. G. S. Berns, J. C. Chappelow, C. F. Zink, G. Pagnoni, M. E. Martin-Skurski, and R. Richards, "Neurobiological Correlates of Social Conformity and Independence During Mental Rotation," *Biological Psychiatry* 58 (2005): 245–253, http://www.ccnl.emory.edu/greg/Berns%20Conformity%20final%20printed.pdf.

21. A. Monk, "The Canadian Model: Invented in South Dakota?" Institutional Investor, August 20, 2013, http://www.institutionalin-vestor.com/blogarticle/3245396/the-canadian-model-invented-in-south-dakota.html.

22. S. Achor, *Before Happiness: The 5 Hidden Keys to Achieving Success, Spreading Happiness, and Sustaining Positive Change* (New York: Crown Publishing / Random House, 2013), 146.

23. There was some contention to this story, but Jeremy Siegel and others who claimed that the Nifty Fifty were never actually was full consensus on which fifty companies were included. As such, any claim that this group underperformed the index of over the long-term is somewhat flawed. See J. Fesenmaier and G. Smith, "The Nifty-Fifty Re-Revisited," *Journal of Investing* 11 no. 3 (2002): 86–90, doi:10.3905/joi.2002.319515.

24. M. J. Mauboussin, *The Success Equation: Untangling Skill and Luck in Business, Sports, and Investing* (Boston, MA: Harvard Business School Publishing, 2012), 21.

25. A. Amit Goyal, and S. Wahal, "The Selection and Termination of Investment Management Firms by Plan Sponsors," *Journal of Finance* 63 no. 4 (2008): 1805–1847.
26. Mauboussin, *The Success Equation*, 22.
27. "In Comes the Waves," *Economist*, June 16, 2005, http://www.economist.com/node/4079027.
28. N. Silver, *The Signal and the Noise* (New York: Penguin, 2012), 22–23.
29. K. J. Knoespel, "Newton's Alchemical Work and the Creation of Economic Value," paper presented at the American Chemical Society's 232nd national meeting in San Francisco, CA, September 11, 2006.
30. T. Levenson, *Newton and the Counterfeiter: The Unknown Detective Career of the World's Greatest Scientist* (New York: Houghton-Mifflin Harcourt, 2010), 243–245.
31. E. Gold and G. Hester, *The Gambler's Fallacy and the Coin's Memory* (unpublished manuscript, Carnegie-Mellon University, Pittsburg, PA, 1989).
32. M. S. Gazzaniga, *Who's in Charge? Free Will and the Science of the Brain* (New York: HarperCollins, 2011), 53–86.
33. G. Wolford, S. E. Newman, M. B. Miller, and G. S. Wig, "Searching for Patterns in Random Sequences," *Canadian Journal of Experimental Psychology* 58, no. 4 (2004): 221–228.
34. P. Gompers, V. Mukharlyamov, and Y. Xuan, "The Cost of Friendship" (NBER working paper 18141) (Cambridge, MA: National Bureau of Economic Research, 2012), accessed August 28, 2013, http://www.nber.org/papers/w18141.pdf.

Part III: The Advisor
1. D. Fernandes, J. G. Lynch, and R. G. Netemeyer, "Financial Literacy, Financial Education and Downstream Financial Behaviors," *Management Science* 60, no. 8 (2014): 1861–1883.

2. P. Slovic, M. L. Finucane, E. Peters, and D. G. MacGregor, "The Affect Heuristic," *European Journal of Operational Research* 177 no. 3 (2007): 1333–1352, doi:10.1016/j.ejor.2005.04.006.

3. D. G. MacGregor, "Imagery and Financial Judgement," *Journal of Psychology and Financial Markets* 3, no. 1 (2002): 15–22, SSRN: http://ssrn.com/abstract=1865423.

4. A. R. Damasio, D. Tranel, and H. Damasio, "Somatic Markers and the Guidance of Behavior: Theory and Preliminary Testing," in *Frontal Lobe Function and Dysfunction*, eds. H. S. Levin, H. M. Eisenberg, and A. L. Benton (New York: Oxford University Press, 1991), 217–229; A. R. Damasio, *The Feeling of What Happens: Body and Emotions in the Making of Consciousness* (Orlando, FL: Mariner Books/Harcourt, 2000).

5. M. Lidsky, I. Rosmarin, J. Rosmarin, and S. Wassyng, *In Search of the Prime Quadrant: The Quest for Better Investment Decisions* (Toronto, Ontario, Canada: Prime Quadrant, 2012), 39–40.

6. Financial Advisor (FA) staff, "Millionaires' Financial Regrets, According to DeVere Group," *FA*, May 30, 2013, http://www.fa-mag.com/news/millionaires—financiial-regrets—according-to-devere-group-14435.html.

7. I. MacNeill, "Hey, Big Spender! Are You Living Beyond Your Means?" *Zoomer Magazine*, December 2012/January 2013, 76–77, http://www.financialtraining.ca/wp-content/uploads/2013/01/Zoomer-money-feature.pdf#.

8. Morningstar and others have suggested that some of the largest mutual funds have an average turnover ratio of nearly 75 percent per year. Source: Mutual Funds Industry—2010; Assessing the Impact of Taxes on Shareholder Return.

9. M. Michael Lewis, "Coach Leach Goes Deep, Very Deep," *New York Times*, December 4, 2005, accessed July 31, 2013, http://www.nytimes.com/2005/12/04/magazine/04coach.html?_r=0&adxnnl=1&pagewanted=all&adxnnlx=1375265141-Ab+Wx/TdEAdbjqTOhK/QDQ.

10. M. J. Mauboussin, *The Success Equation: Untangling Skill and Luck in Business, Sports, and Investing* (Boston, MA: Harvard Business School Publishing, 2005), 23.

11. W. L. Winston, *Mathletics: How Gamblers, Managers, and Sports Enthusiasts Use Mathematics in Baseball, Basketball, and Football* (Princeton, NJ: Princeton University Press, 2009), 229–232.

12. G. P. Brinson, L. R. Hood, and G. L. Beebower, "Determinants of Portfolio Performance," *Financial Analysts Journal* 42, no. 4 (1986): 39–48.

13. E. F. Fama Jr., speech at the 1997 Dimensional Fund Advisors' Conference, University of Chicago Graduate School of Business, Chicago, Illinois, 1997, cited in Index Fund Advisors, "Quotes," 1999, https://www.ifa.com/quotes/.

14. Lidsky et al., *In Search of the Prime Quadrant*, 90.

15. H. Marks, *The Most Important Thing: Uncommon Sense for the Thoughtful Investor* (New York: Columbia University Press, 2011), 44–45.

16. Mauboussin, *The Success Equation*.

17. D. Hume, *An Enquiry Concerning Human Understanding*, ed. T. L. Beauchamp (Oxford, UK: Clarendon Press, 2000).

18. B. Russell, *The Problems of Philosophy* (Oxford, UK: Oxford University Press, 1959).

19. D. Kahneman, *Thinking Fast, Thinking Slow* (New York: Farrar, Straus, and Giroux, 2011).

20. A. K. Barnett-Hart, "The Story of the CDO Market Meltdown: An Empirical Analysis," (thesis, Harvard College, Cambridge, MA, 2009), http://www.hks.harvard.edu/m-rcbg/students/dunlop/2009-CDOmeltdown.pdf.

21. N. Silver, *The Signal and the Noise* (New York: Penguin, 2012), 30.

22. Robert J. Shiller, *Irrational Exuberance*, 2nd edition (New York: Broadway Books / Random House, 2015), 20.

23. J. Zweig, *Your Money and Your Brain: How the New Science of Neuroeconomics Can Help Make You Rich* (New York: Simon and Schuster, 2007), 93.

24. Ibid.

25. Ibid.

26. M. Kilka and M. Weber, "Home Bias in International Stock Return Expectations," *Journal of Psychology and Financial Markets* 1 no. 3–4 (2000): 176–192, doi:10.1207/S15327760JPFM0134_3.

27. P. Kenning, P. Mohr, S. Erk, H. Walter, and H. Plassmann, "The Role of Fear in Home-Biased Decision Making: First Insights from Neuroeconomics. (MPRA working paper 1076) (Munich, Germany: University Library of Munich, 2006), http://mpra.ub.uni-muenchen.de/1076/1/.

28. S&P/TSX composites focusing on resource stocks makes our asset markets swing in tune to emerging markets, *not* the G7 developed ones. S&P/TSX bears no resemblance to the Canadian economy—industries' contributions to GDP are not necessarily proportionally weighted in markets. See S. Barlow, "The Strange Case of Dr. Economy and Mr. Market," *Globe and Mail*, March 5, 2013, http://penny2.theglobeandmail.com/servlet/ArticleNews/story/gam/20130305/RBINSIGHTJEKYLLHYDE0304ATL.

29. J. Zweig, "Did You Beat the Market?" *Fundamentalist* (January 2000): 55–57, http://money.cnn.com/magazines/moneymag/moneymagarchive/2000/01/01/271477/.

30. Interestingly enough, despite this, average private equity returns, net of fees, are just about equal to the results of the S&P 500. See S. N. Kaplan and A. Schoar, "Private Equity Performance: Returns, Persistence and Capital Flows," (MIT Sloan working paper 4446-03; AFA; 2004), San Diego meetings, http://ssrn.com/abstract=473341.

31. J. Schlegel, "Single Malt, Many Paybacks," *Private Wealth*, January 4, 2013, http://www.fa-mag.com/news/single-malt—many-paybacks-12977.html.

32. A. Gopnik, A. Meltzoff, and P. Kuhl, *The Scientist in the Crib: What Early Learning Tells Us About the Mind* (New York: First Perennial, 2001), 186–87.

33. J. LeDoux, *Synaptic Self: How Our Brains Become Who We Are* (New York: Viking Press, 2002), 79–81.

34. R. Aunger, *The Electric Meme: A New Theory of How We Think* (New York: Free Press, 2002), 185.

35. M. J. Mauboussin, *More Than You Know: Finding Financial Wisdom in Unconventional Places* (New York: Columbia University Press, 2013), 135.

36. C. Heath and D. Heath, *Decisive: How to Make Better Choices in Life and Work* (New York: Crown Business / Random House, 2014), 58.

37. Marks, *The Most Important Thing*, 101.

38. R. Dobelli, *The Art of Thinking Clearly* (New York: Harper Collins Publishers, 2013), 303.

39. S. P. Dow, A. Glassco, J. Kass, M. Schwarz, D. L. Schwartz, and S. R. Klemmer, "Parallel Prototyping Leads to Better Design Results, More Divergence, and Increased Self Efficacy," *Transactions on Computer-Human Interaction* 17, no. 4 (2010): 18–23, cited in Heath and Heath, *Decisive*, 53.

40. B. Scheibehenne, R. Greifeneder, and P. M. Todd, "Can There Ever Be Too Many Options? A Meta-Analytic Review of Choice Overload," *Journal of Consumer Research* 37 (2010): 409–425, cited in Heath and Heath, *Decisive*, 282.

41. K. M. Eisenhardt, "Making Fast Strategic Decisions in High-Velocity Environments," *Academy of Management Journal* 32 (1989): 543–576, http://www.jstor.org/stable/256434.

42. M. Gladwell, *Blink: The Power of Thinking without Thinking* (New York: Little, Brown / Time Warner, 2000).

43. C. H. Park and S. H. Irwin, "The Profitability of Technical Analysis: A Review" (AgMAS project research report 2004-04, 2004), http://www.farmdoc.illinois.edu/marketing/agmas/reports/04_04/AgMAS04_04.pdf.

44. P. L. Bernstein, *Capital Ideas: Improbable Origins of Modern Wall Street* (New York: Free Press, 1993), 126–127; E. F. Fama, "My Life in Finance," *Annual Review of Financial Economics* 3, no. 1 (2010): 1–15, doi:10.1146/annurev-financial-102710-144858.

45. M. Hulbert, "Newsletter Returns: Be Skeptical," *Barron's*, October 3, 2013, http://online.barrons.com/article/SB50001424053 11190332060457910952164286630.html.

46. Murray Stahl's *Collected Commentaries and Conundrums Regarding Value Investing*, third edition, vol. 1. Murray Stahl's *Collected Commentaries and Conundrums Regarding Value Investing*, third edition, vol. 1 [OOP] includes *How They Did It: Exceptional Stories of Great Investors* (Hammond, IN: Horizon Publishing, 2011).

47. W. Samuelson and R. Zeckhauser, "Status Quo Bias in Decision Making," *Journal of Risk and Uncertainty* 1 (1988): 7–59, accessed October 27, 2013, http://www.hks.harvard.edu/fs/rzeckhau/SQBDM.pdf.

48. O. S. Mitchell, G. R. Mottola, S. P. Utkus, and T. Yamaguchi, "The Inattentive Participant: Portfolio Trading Behavior in 401(k) Plans" (PRC working paper 2006-2, 2006) (Philadelphia, PA: Pension Research Council, 2006), https://www.aeaweb.org/assa/2006/0108_1300_0902.pdf.

49. E. J. Johnson and D. G. Goldstein, "Defaults and Donation Decisions," *Transplantation* 78, no. 12 (2004): 1713–1716, https://www0.gsb.columbia.edu/mygsb/faculty/research/pub-files/1139/Defaults_and_Donation_Decisions_-_Transplantation.pdf.

50. V. Niederhoffer, *The Education of a Speculator* (Hoboken, NJ: John Wiley, 1998).

51. Ibid., 156.

52. J. Bogel, *The Clash of the Cultures* (Hoboken, NJ: John Wiley, 2012), 302–307.

53. Heath and Heath, *Decisive*, 14.

54. L. Clamen, *The Best Investment Advice I Ever Received* (New York: Warner Business / Hachette, 2006), 116.

55. D. Kahneman, J. L. Knetsch, and R. H. Thaler, "Experimental Tests of the Endowment Effect and the Coase Theorem," *Journal of Political Economy* 98 no. 6 (1990):1325–1348, http://www.jstor.org/stable/2937761.

56. Financial Times Stock Exchange (FTSE) Rural Advancement Foundation International (RAFI®), *FTSE RAFI Index Series: Staggered Rebalancing,* 2012, http://www.ftse.com/products/downloads/FTSE-RAFI-Staggered-Rebalancing-Paper.pdf.

Part IV: The Price of Advice

1. C. Heath and D. Heath, *Switch: How to Change Things When Change Is Hard* (Toronto, Ontario, Canada: Random House of Canada, 2010), 87–93.

2. Ascentum, *Strengthening Investor Protection in Ontario Speaking with Ontarians* (Toronto, Ontario, Canada: Ontario Securities Commission/Investor Education Fund, 2013), accessed August 28, 2013, https://www.osc.gov.on.ca/documents/en/Investors/iap_20130318_strengthening-investor-protection.pdf.

3. J. M. Brown, "Incentives Matter," *Reformed Broker*, June 3, 2014, http://thereformedbroker.com/2014/06/03/incentives-matter/?+thereformedbroker+%28http%3A%2F%2Fthereformedbroker.com%2Ffeed%29.

4. United States White House, Presidential Commission, *The Effects of Conflicted Investment Advice on Retirement Savings. Report to the Executive Office of the President of the United States* (Washington, DC: Author, 2015), https://www.whitehouse.gov/sites/default/files/docs/cea_coi_report_final.pdf; and Brent, (2013); "Don't Let High Management Fees Drain Your Portfolio," *Globe and Mail*, November 22, 2013, http://www.theglobeandmail.com/globe-investor/funds-and-etfs/etfs/high-management-costs-drain-away-portfolio-growth/article15561239/.

5. J. Daw, "Industry Defends Mutual Fund Trailer Fees," *Star*, August 11, 2010, accessed September 1, 2013, http://www.thestar.

com/business/2010/08/11/daw_industry_defends_mutual_fund_tra
iler_fees.html.

6. J. Davis, "Reveal the 'True Cost' of the Croupier's Take," *Financial Times*, March 21, 2010, accessed September 3, 2013,
http://www.independentinvestor.info/PDF-Downloads/ETF-
MUTUAL-FUNDS-WRAP-ACCOUNTS-FUNDS-08/doc.1825-
%20Davis%20FT.com%202010%20Apparent%20vs%20real%20
mutual%20fund%20expenses.pdf.

7. Charles D. Ellis, "Will Business Success Spoil the Investment
Management Profession?" *Journal of Portfolio Management* 27, no. 3
(2001): 11–15, doi:10.3905/jpm.2001.319797.

8. K. Fitz-Gerald, *Fiscal Hangover: How to Profit from the New
Global Economy* (Hoboken, NJ: John Wiley, 2009), 283–284; K. J.
Johnson and T. M. Krueger, "Market Timing versus Dollar-Cost
Averaging: Evidence Based on Two Decades of Standard & Poor's
500 Index Values," *Journal of the Academy of Finance* 2, no. 2
(2004): 24–34.

9. D. Kahneman and D. T. Miller, "Norm Theory: Comparing
Reality to its Alternatives," *Psychological Review* 93, no. 2 (1986):
136–153, doi:10.1037/0033-295X.93.2.136.

10. M. Bar-Eli, O. H. Azar, I. Ritov, Y. Keidar-Levin, and G.
Schein, "Action Bias among Elite Soccer Goalkeepers: The Case of
Penalty Kicks," *Journal of Economic Psychology* 28, no. 5 (2005):
606–621, doi:10.1016/j.joep.2006.12.001.

11. S. D. Stewart, J. J. Neumann, C. R. Knittel, and J. Heisler,
"Absence of Value: An Analysis of Investment Allocation Decisions
by Institutional Plan Sponsors," *Financial Analysts Journal* 65 no. 6
(2009): 34–51, http://www.rijpm.com/pre_reading_files/
Scott_Stewart.pdf.

12. B. M. Barber and T. Odean, "Trading Is Hazardous to Your
Wealth: The Common Stock Investment Performance of Individual
Investors," *Journal of Finance* 55, no. 2 (2000): 773–806,
http://www.independentinvestor.info/PDF-Downloads/HOW-TO-
INVEST-RETURNS-INDEXES-02/doc.2209D-%20Odean%20

barber%202000%20trading%20is%20hazardous%20SSRN-id219228.pdf.

13. Ibid.

14. J. Bogel, *Common Sense on Mutual Funds* (Hoboken, NJ: John Wiley, 1999), 92.

15. Canadian Foundation for Advancement of Investor Rights (FAIR), *Canadian Money Market Funds—Zero Returns* (Toronto, Ontario, Canada: Author, 2010), http://faircanada.ca/wp-content/uploads/2010/03/MMF-Report-March-11-Final.pdf.

Part V: The Measures of Success

1. C. Ellis, *Winning the Loser's Game: Timeless Strategies for Successful Investing*, 4th edition (New York: McGraw-Hill, 2002), 5.

2. J. J. Siegel, *Stocks for the Long Run* (New York: McGraw-Hill, 1998), 253, 272–277.

3. E. F. Fama, "The Behavior of Stock-Market Prices," *Journal of Business* 38, no. 1 (1965): 34–105, http://www.jstor.org/stable/2350752.

4. According to Dorsey Wright & Associates (n.d.), "98 percent of those top managers [in the 1990s] had periods of underperformance extending three years or more. 98 percent is not a misprint! Even more striking, 68 percent of the top managers ended up in the bottom quartile for some three-year period and a full 40 percent of them visited the bottom decile during that ten years" (p. 1). See Dorsey Wright, "Point and Figure Special Report: Ouch! What to Do after a Bad Quarter," Money Management, http://dorsey-wrightmm.com/downloads/hrs_research/Point%20and%20Figure%20Special%20Report.pdf. See also Buttonwood, "Reliably Unreliable," *Economist*, December 12, 2014, http://www.economist.com/blogs/buttonwood/2014/12/picking-funds.

5. [i] Gilles Hilary and Lior Menzly, "Does Past Success Lead Analysts to Become Overconfident?" *Management Science* 52, no. 4 (2006).

6. A. Dürer, "Untangling Skill and Luck: How to Think About Outcomes—Past, Present, and Future" *Legg Mason*, July 15, 2010 http://contenta.mkt1710.com/lp/26966/115068/Untangling%20S kill%20and%20Luck.pdf

7. A. Rappaport and M. J. Mauboussin, "Does It Pay to Be an Active Investor?" Expectations Investing, 2001, http://www.expecta-tionsinvesting.com/pdf/active.pdf.

8. M. Wheeler, "The Luck Factor in Great Decisions," *Harvard Business Review*, November 18, 2013, http://blogs.hbr.org/2013/11/the-luck-factor-in-great-decisions/.

9. "Ashes to Ashes, Funds to Funds," *Bloomberg Businessweek*, September 29, 1991, http://www.bloomberg.com/bw/stories/1991-09-29/ashes-to-ashes-funds-to-funds.

10. Ibid.

11. D. Kruger, "Booby Prize," *Forbes*, September 20, 2004, http://www.forbes.com/forbes/2004/0920/246.html.

12. M. S. Gazzaniga, "The Split Brain Revisited," *Scientific American*, July 1998, 50–55, http://www.utdallas.edu/~otoole/CGS2301_S09/7_split_brain.pdf.

13. David Leinweber, *Nerds on Wall Street: Math, Machines and Wired Markets* (Hoboken, NJ: John Wiley, 2009), 137–140.

14. This is one of the quotations that has been widely attributed to Twain, but there is no specific source confirming that it actually for this came from him. Jeff Sommer, "Funny, but I've Heard This Market Song Before," *New York Times*, June 18, 2011.

15. P. Fraser, "How Do U.S. and Japanese Investors Process Information and How Do They Form Their Expectations of the Future? Evidence From Quantitative Survey Based Data" (working paper 00-14, 2000) (Aberdeen, UK: University of Aberdeen, Aberdeen Papers in Accountancy, Finance and Management), http://dx.doi.org/10.2139/ssrn.257440.

16. Ellis, *Winning the Loser's Game*, 73.

17. Mauboussin, *The Success Equation*, 3.

18. Mauboussin, *The Success Equation*; N. Silver, *The Signal and the Noise* (New York: Penguin, 2012).

19. M. J. Mauboussin, *More Than You Know: Finding Financial Wisdom in Unconventional Places* (New York: Columbia University Press, 2013), 47.

20. A. Mauboussin and S. Arbesman, "Differentiating Skill and Luck in Financial Markets" (working paper, 2011), http://dx.doi.org/10.2139/ssrn.1664031.

21. A. Tversky and D. Kahneman, "Belief in the Law of Small Numbers," *Psychological Bulletin* 76, no. 2 (1971): 105–110.

22. M. T. Rogan, K. S. Leon, D. L. Perez, and E. R. Kandel, "Distinct Neural Signatures for Safety and Danger in the Amygdala and Striatum of the Mouse," *Neuron* 46, no. 2 (2005): 309–320, PubMed PMID: 15848808.

23. J. Brennan, *Straight Talk on Investing: What You Need to Know* (Hoboken, NJ: Fisher Investments / John Wiley, 2002), 178.

24. R. F. Harrod, *The Life of John Maynard Keynes* (London: Macmillan, 1951).

25. K. L. Fisher and L. Hoffmans, *Markets Never Forget (But People Do): How Your Memory Is Costing You Money and Why This Time Isn't Different* (Hoboken, NJ: Fisher Investments / John Wiley, 2011), 3.

26. K. L. Fisher and L. Hoffmans, *Debunkery: Learn It, Do It, and Profit from It—Seeing Through Wall Street's Money-Killing Myths* (Hoboken, NJ: Fisher Investments / John Wiley, 2011), 92–97.

27. Matthew Rice and Geoff Strotman, "An analysis of manager performance, consistency, and persistency: The Next Chapter in the Active vs. Passive Management Debate" (white paper, March 2007), DiMeo Schneider & Associates; "The Truth About Top-Performing Money Managers Why Investors Should Expect—and Accept—Periods of Poor Relative Performance," Baird's Advisory Services Research, http://content.rwbaird.com/RWB/Content/PDF/Insights/Whitepapers/Truth-About-Top-Performing-Money-Managers.pdf.

28. L. Clamen, *The Best Investment Advice I Ever Received* (New York: Warner Business /Hachette, 2006), 73.

29. W. N. Goetzmann and N. Peles, "Cognitive Dissonance and Mutual Fund Investors," *Journal of Financial Research* 20, no. 2 (1997): 145–158, accessed October 15, 2013, http://citeseerx.ist.psu.edu/viewdoc/download?doi=10.1.1.17.4713 &rep=rep1&type=pdf.

30. R. H. Thaler, A. Tversky, D. Kahneman, and A. Schwartz, "The Effect of Myopia and Loss Aversion on Risk Taking: An Experimental Test," *Quarterly Journal of Economics* 112, no. 2 (1997): 647–61, doi:10.1162/003355397555226.

31. D. Goodgame, "The Game of Risk: How the Best Golfer in the World Got Even Better," *Time*, August 14, 2000, cited in Mauboussin, *More Than You Know*, 135, 153–154.

32. R. M. Sapolsky, *Why Zebras Don't Get Ulcers* (New York: Henry Holt, 1994), 4–13.

33. S. Frederick, G. Loewenstein, and T. O'Donoghue, "Time Discounting and Time Preference: A Critical Review," *Journal of Economic Literature* 40 (2002): 350–401, http://www.cmu.edu/dietrich/sds/docs/loewenstein/TimeDiscounting.pdf.

Part VI: Expectations

1. P. L. Bernstein, "Where, Oh Where are the .400 Hitters of Yesteryear?" *Financial Analysts Journal* 54, no. 6 (1999): 6–14, http://dx.doi.org/10.2469/faj.v55.n2.2254.

2. C. H. Fine, *Clockspeed: Winning Industry Control in the Age of Temporary Advantage* (Reading, MA: Perseus Books, 1998).

3. S. Ramo, *Extraordinary Tennis for the Ordinary Player* (New York: Crown Publishers, 1977).

4. C. Ellis, *Winning the Loser's Game: Timeless Strategies for Successful Investing*, 4th edition (New York: McGraw-Hill, 2002), 5–7.

5. M. Hulbert, "Man vs. Machine: The Great Stock Showdown," *Wall Street Journal*, May 10, 2013, accessed July 10, 2013, http://online.wsj.com/article/SB1000142412788732405970457847 1154109438438.html?mod=rss_mobile_uber_feed.

6. Ibid.

7. M. Gladwell, *David and Goliath: Underdogs, Misfits, and the Art of Battling Giants* (New York: Little, Brown /Hachette, 2015).

8. J. C. Bogle, *Common Sense on Mutual Funds: Fully Updated 10th Anniversary Issue* (Hoboken, NJ: John Wiley, 2010), 354–371.

9. M. J. Mauboussin, *More Than You Know: Finding Financial Wisdom in Unconventional Places* (New York: Columbia University Press, 2013), 239–242.

10. Corporate Strategy Board, *Stall Points: Barriers to Growth for the Large Corporate Enterprise* (Arlington, VA: Strategy Leadership Council, 1998).

11. J. Strasbourg and M. Gongloff, "Soros's Ex-Manager to Close Shop," *Wall Street Journal*, August 19, 2010, accessed September 8, 2013, http://online.wsj.com/article/SB10001424052748703649004575437461858678850.html.

12. S. Ro, "Stock Market Investors Have Become Absurdly Impatient," *Business Insider*, August 7, 2012, http://www.businessinsider.com/stock-investor-holding-period-2012-8.

13. P. Domm, "False Rumor of Explosion at White House Causes Stocks to Briefly Plunge; AP Confirms Its Twitter Feed Was Hacked," CNBC Market Insider, April 23, 2013, http://www.cnbc.com/ id/100646197.

14. I. Ben-David, F. A. Franzoni, and R. Moussawi, "Do ETFs Increase Volatility?" (NBER working paper 20071) (Cambridge, MA: National Bureau of Economic Research, 2014), http://www.nber.org/papers/w20071.pdf.

15. Barry Ritholtz, "How You, the Amateur Investor, Can Beat the Pros," November 6, 2015, https://www.washingtonpost.com/business/get-there/how-you-the-amateur-investor-can-beat-the-pros/2015/11/06/2c1daed0-8430-11e5-8ba6-cec48b74b2a7_print.html.

16. H. F. Chua, J. E. Boland, and R. E. Nisbett, "Cultural Variation in Eye Movements During Scene Perception," *Proceedings of the*

National Academy of Sciences 102, no. 35 (2005): 12629–12633, cited in N. Hertz, *Eyes Wide Open: How to Make Smart Decisions in a Confusing World* (New York: Harper Collins, 2013), 21–22.

17. J. Zweig, "Lesson From Buffett: Doubt Yourself," *Wall Street Journal*, May 5, 2013, http://www.wsj.com/news/articles/SB10001424127887323687604 578465092347394804?mod=WSJ_article_RecentColumns_TheIn-telligentInvestor.

18. I. E. Hyman Jr., S. M. Boss, M. W. Breanne, K. E. McKenzie, and J. M. Caggiano, "Did You See the Unicycling Clown? Inatten-tional Blindness while Walking and Talking on a Cell Phone," *Applied Cognitive Psychology* 24 (2010): 597–607.

19. Maria Konnikova, "Multitask Masters," *New Yorker*, May 7, 2014, http://www.newyorker.com/science/maria-konnikova/multi-task-masters.

Lightning Source UK Ltd.
Milton Keynes UK
UKHW020228080122
396806UK00009B/438/J